EMMA
HAMILTON

EMMA HAMILTON

Norah Lofts

Coward, McCann & Geoghegan, Inc.

New York

First American Edition
Copyright © 1978 by Norah Lofts

Library of Congress Cataloging in Publication Data:

Lofts, Norah Robinson,
    Emma Hamilton.

    1. Hamilton, Emma, Lady, 1761?–1815.
2. Mistresses – England – Biography. 3. Nelson,
Horatio Nelson, Viscount, 1758–1805.
DA483.H3L63 1978   941.07'3'0924 [B]   77–26868
ISBN 0-698-10912-0

This book was designed and produced in Great Britain by
George Rainbird Ltd,
36 Park Street,
London W1Y 4DE, England

House Editor: Felicity Luard
Assistant House Editor: Jane Collins
Designer: Pauline Harrison
Picture Researcher: Barbara Fraser
Indexer: Myra Clark

Text set by SX Composing Ltd, Leigh-on-Sea, Essex, England.
Printed and bound by Dai Nippon Printing Co. Ltd, Tokyo, Japan.

(frontispiece) Lady Hamilton as a Bacchante engraved by
R. J. Smith after a painting by Sir Joshua Reynolds.

Contents

Color Plates

*The page numbers given are those opposite
the color plates, or, in the case of a double page spread,
those either side of the plate.*

CHAPTER

1

Emily Lyon, Emma Hart

I own through distress my
virtue was vanquished but my
sense of virtue was not over-
come.

Emma to Romney

To begin at the beginning is a sound rule, but sometimes one that is rather hard to follow, for the origins of those born into obscurity are often very obscure indeed.

When the wife of a North Country blacksmith gave birth to a daughter the event seemed of little importance. Even now authorities vary about the date; some use question marks or the small *c.* which indicates uncertainty; some give her birthday as 12th of May; some as 6th of April: she herself always celebrated her birthday on 26th of April. Only one of the many people who loved her seems to have cared to probe farther and was sent copies of entries in the Neston parish register; her parents Henry Lyon and Mary Kidd were married in the church there in June 1764 and she was baptized in April 1765. She was given the name of Emily. Both her parents were illiterate, making their mark instead of signing their names. Her mother in later life acquired enough education to write coherent and sensible letters.

Henry Lyon died before his daughter was a year old. His widow went to work; there is mention of dressmaking, and of domestic service; and the child was brought up by her grandmother Kidd in the Flintshire village of Hawarden. That she was happy is

(previous page) Emma was born in a Cheshire country village in April 1765.

10

proved by her attitude towards her grandmother, her mother and her numerous cousins; and also by her own disposition. It is rare for children who feel neglected or deprived to develop into exhuberant, self-confident extroverts. And she was certainly well-fed, her looks prove that. Malnutrition in childhood leaves scars – flat noses, bad teeth, bowlegs, knobbly joints. Whatever else in her story may be debatable, her beauty cannot be questioned. She had hair of a shade between golden and auburn, which when let loose, rippled down to her heels, large blue-grey eyes of exceptional brilliance, one of them marred, or enhanced, by a brown speck, said to vary with her mood, and a complexion which somebody likened to apple blossom. And hers was no static beauty; any emotion, genuine or assumed was reflected in her face. Romney, who at the height of his fame could ask £1,500 for a portrait painted her, or pictures inspired by her, thirty – some say fifty – times.

The first person to wish to draw her – to catch forever something of beauty was a Miss Thomas, the daughter of her first employer. Like all poor girls Emily went early to work; and it may be that the experiences and changes crammed into so few years misled people into thinking that she was older than she was. All people

Her father was an illiterate blacksmith in Neston, Cheshire.

11

Little Emma, thought to be Emma painted as a child by Charles Greville. Her daughter by Greville was also known as 'Little Emma'.

matured earlier in the eighteenth century than they do today, and the poor matured earlier than the more sheltered. If Emily first went to work as a nursemaid at the age of thirteen, she was luckier than most, who went into service at the age of eleven or twelve; and she had, even then, a relatively easy job; nursemaid.

She did not hold it long. It is assumed that her mother found work in London, and that Emily went, too.

Why did they both change their names? There is no reliable answer. Out of the obscurity, Emily Lyon emerges as Emma Hart, and her mother as Mrs Cadogan. There is no evidence that either change was brought about by marriage; and since their relationship, mother and daughter, was always acknowledged and they were to be closely associated until the elder woman died, it would have seemed rational for them to have assumed the same name.

Mrs Cadogan was the name assumed
by Emma's mother, née Mary Kidd.
Until her death in 1810,
she acted as Emma's housekeeper,
and was her staunchest companion,
the one person who knew all about her,
the one before whom no
attitude was needed.

Cadogan has undertones of grandeur, Hart is commonplace. It is just possible that something had happened, something from which they both wished to dissociate themselves and that a temporary lack of contact made them change names without consulting each other. The changes were accepted with – from a biographical point of view – a deplorable lack of curiosity. Even the Honourable Charles Francis Greville who took the trouble to have the Neston parish register consulted so that Emma's age might be ascertained, appears never to have asked how, or why, Mary Lyon had become Mary Cadogan, and her daughter, Emma Hart. Grandmother Kidd and all the rest of the family in and around Hawarden, seemed equally incurious.

Emma had no difficulty in obtaining employment in London. Girls from the country were favoured by employers; they were less likely to have hungry families waiting for handouts at the kitchen door; they enjoyed better health, had probably already survived the cowpox, which Dr Jenner had proved to be a guard against smallpox, and they were regarded as comparatively innocent and therefore more moral. Emma's first known job in London was as nursemaid in the household of Dr Richard Budd where one of her fellow servants was Jane Powell, later to become a famous actress.

Friendship with Jane may have helped to develop Emma's latent histrionic talent, which came to full flower in her famous Attitudes. Thousands of people played the parlour game of *tableaux vivants*, the striking and holding of a pose, but Emma's were to be something special; with no scenery and no properties except two shawls she could portray any character, any emotion. It is pleasant to imagine two young girls, both destined for fame, practising the art of acting in the attic bedrooms of Dr Budd's house.

Emma was not there long and there followed a space of time over which obscurity falls again, breeding myth and legend and rumour. The Prince Regent liked to say that he had seen her, wearing wooden pattens and selling flowers, but what he said was notoriously unreliable – he liked to say that he was present at the Battle of Waterloo, which he was not. She is said to have been a shop assistant, a barmaid, a parlourmaid, a companion to a woman of ill-repute, to have been on the streets herself. One rather doubts the last-named occupation. She was never promiscuous. She was beautiful and possessed in large measure the quality which another age was to call sex appeal but her life on the whole follows an all-over pattern – one man at a time. She said of herself that though not virtuous, she always had virtue in her; and if, as some cynic said, virtue largely consists of a lack of temptation, the virtue within her must have been strong, for the temptations must have been enormous.

The next positive thing known about her was that she was working for a man known as Dr Graham, half quack, half mystic in a remarkable establishment known as The Temple of Aeschlapius in the Adelphi.

People at the end of the eighteenth century were inquisitive, credulous, and like the Athenians of whom St Paul complained, always ready to run after any new thing. Dr Graham offered many new things, some genuine, some fraudulent. Treatment by electricity and by mud-baths – derided by his detractors in his day – the power of prayer, of hypnotism and of suggestibility, have all since been recognized. Dr Graham had such a belief in prayer that when George III fell ill, he wrote a prayer on paper and asked that it should be pinned to the King's pillow. Did he have equal faith in his so-called Celestial Bed, hired out at £50 a session to hitherto barren couples and practically guaranteed to bring conception?

Sex, overt or indirect was the keynote of the Temple, how to retain or regain youth, beauty, fertility. Dr Graham spared no expense; all the rooms in which people waited for a consultation,

Emma posed among marble statues,
lightly clad as the Goddess Hygeia,
while working in Dr Graham's Temple of Aeschlapius
at the Adelphi. Rowlandson drew his cartoon
some years afterward in about 1800.

or a session in the Celestial Bed, or a sermon, were lavishly furnished, provided with soft lights and sweet music. There was a statue, considered beautiful even by Dr Graham's critics, of the Goddess of Plenty with her cornucopia overflowing and beautiful young children surrounding her.

It is possible that Emma Hart joined this establishment as a singer; she had a good, as-yet-untrained voice and she loved to sing. She may have helped, when not singing, to sell some of Dr Graham's nostrums, especially his Nervous Balsam, a panacea for almost anything but a broken bone. Sometimes, among the dead marble girls she posed, lightly draped in filmy classical-style clothes as the Goddess Hygeia. The Temple became one of the sights of London, all the fashionable world must visit it, if only from curiosity and to be on display there was to invite the attention of men in search of a mistress.

To say that the finding of a rich protector was the aim of many poor pretty girls at the time is not to criticize the age, and even less the girls themselves. Life for the poor was very harsh and insecure and the opportunities of rising out of the slough of poverty by honest means were few; for a poor girl there was no chance of education, no profession open, save the oldest of all. To be a rich man's pet for as long as one's looks lasted, to get as many gifts as possible and save a little here and there, perhaps even, if one were very lucky, to receive a generous parting present or a small pension, was a very usual ambition among girls who had no endowment but their looks.

Emma's beauty began to flower in an uninhibited age. The ultrarespectability, with the accompanying hypocrisy, of Victorian times had not yet clamped down. Many men openly kept mistresses, some flaunted them, prized them as they prized their blood horses and hounds of high pedigree. To have a mistress was fashionable. One Continental monarch, fortunate enough to love his wife, kept a mistress purely for show and paraded her, splendidly clad and wonderfully bejewelled, and serving no other purpose at all.

(opposite) Emma as *The Spinstress* by Romney, commissioned by Charles Greville in 1782. It was not completed until after Emma had gone to Naples in 1786, so he never bought it – an unwise decision as it is regarded as Romney's finest work.

George III, King of England, married and as strict as only a reformed rake could be, had had a mistress in his time. All his sons had mistresses; the Prince of Wales had several, though only one, Mrs Fitzherbert is much remembered; the Duke of Clarence was faithful to his Mrs Jordan; the Duke of Kent truly loved his Madame de Laurent, and only parted from her for dynastic reasons – his marriage resulted in the birth of Victoria; and the Duke of Sussex had his Mrs Bugge. The mistress, the kept woman, was a perfectly acceptable part of the social structure, so long as certain conventions were observed. Decently married women and innocent young girls could not be expected to receive, or to visit a woman who had lost her reputation. Actually, Emma, in becoming the mistress of Sir Harry Fetherstonhaugh, of Up Park in Sussex, was no more blameworthy than beauties of a later day, with their marriages and divorces, and remarriages, all aimed at publicity.

But she had chosen badly. Sir Harry was not the ideal protector for a girl who though ignorant, was eager to learn. He was a typical country squire, hearty and hospitable, possibly even then, stupid. Later he was to be referred to as silly old man. At Up Park, Emma learned little except horsemanship, for which she showed a natural ability. And the riding habit of the day, with, apart from the skirt, a jaunty touch of masculinity about it, would suit a slender sixteen-year-old figure. Pretty, high-spirited, quick-witted, she was much admired by the men who visited Up Park to enjoy Sir Harry's hospitality and to shoot his pheasants.

Among his guests was the Honourable Charles Francis Greville. He was a son of the Earl of Warwick, but a younger son with no estate of his own, merely an allowance of between £500 and £600 a year from his father. This income he eked out by holding various minor government posts. He would certainly be glad to go to Up Park for the shooting, though he would probably have found the hilarious, bucolic company little to his taste. He was thirty-one years old by the calendar but born old by nature, cool, dry, cynical, pedantic, a scholar, an aesthete, a man whose most

(opposite) Up Park by Tillemans, the country seat of Sir Harry Featherstonhaugh in Sussex, where Emma spent a summer of great gaiety in 1781 as Sir Harry's mistress.

(above) Amateur theatricals were among the entertainments at Up Park. In this painting, Emma is on the left, with an unknown actor-manager and actress.
(opposite) Sir Harry Featherstonhaugh of Up Park, painted by Pompeo Battoni while in Rome during his Grand Tour, five years before Emma became his mistress for a brief space in 1781. He was a typical country squire, hearty and hospitable, possibly even then, stupid.

intimate friend was his uncle, Sir William Hamilton, twenty years his senior.

Greville would certainly notice Emma for he was a connoisseur of beautiful things, and so far as his means allowed, a collector. Emma noticed him, perhaps because of his difference from the other guests. The attraction of opposites is a cliché; but one person who admired Emma in later days said that in some ways her mind was masculine, and Charles Greville certainly had an old-maidish streak – his house is described as 'dainty'.

Exactly what happened at Up Park in the autumn of 1781 is not recorded, but in December Sir Harry turned her out, knowing that she was penniless, and pregnant. There is no other evidence to show that he was more callous than average, and when he eventually married he chose his dairymaid and treated her and her family kindly, so Emma must have offended him deeply and

given him good reason to suspect that he was not the father of the child.

In January 1782, Emma wrote to Greville, and the wrapper on the letter could only have been given to her by him; it was franked – that is given free passage by mail, one of the perks of government office – and addressed to him in his own elegant writing; moreover it began 'Yesterday did I receve your kind letter . . .' So he had been writing to her, and providing her with the means of writing to him. Possibly Sir Harry's suspicion was justified.

In later life Emma said that her education did not begin until she was seventeen; but at sixteen she could write, not well – she never did. To the end her spelling was highly idiosyncratic, and her punctuation eccentric. (She was not alone in this; people with far more formal education made slips so that later writers, quoting, feel obliged to put *sic* in brackets.) In many of Emma's letters the irregularity of her punctuation gave a breathless urgency, and she never wrote a more urgent one than the one which Charles Greville received on the 10th of January 1782.

> . . . believe me I am allmost distracktid I have never hard from Sir H . . . what shall I dow good god what shall I dow I have wrote 7 letters and no anser I cant come to town for want of mony I have not a farthing to bless my self with . . . O G what shall I dow What shall I dow . . . O G that I was in your posesion as I was in Sir H what a happy girl would I have been girl indeed, or what else am I but a girl in distres in reall distress for gods sake G write the minet you get this and only tell me what I ham to dow Derect some whay I am allmos mad O for gods sake tell me what is to become on me O dear Grevell write to me Write to me G adue and believe yours for ever Emly Hart

One stands back and observes that she does not, in this desperate letter, feel the need to mention the reason for her distress. Greville *knew*.

(opposite) The Honourable Charles Francis Greville (fourth from left at a meeting of the Dilettanti Society) was, like his uncle Sir William Hamilton, a connoisseur of beautiful things. He added Emma to his collection at minimum expense, after Sir Harry had cast her out, six months pregnant and 'in reall distress'.
(inset opposite) Greville painted by Romney in 1781, the year he met Emma at Up Park.

His reply was chilly, ponderous, pompous. He advised her to repair the breach with Sir Harry, and then added – 'I have never seen a woman clever enough to keep a man who was tired of her.' He explained that if reconciliation were not brought about and Emily came to live with him he would not trouble himself about any of her family – except her mother – nor with any acquaintances she had made at Up Park. Then he relented a little and promised that the child should never want; and that he was sending some money. 'Do not throw it away.' Toward the end of the long, minatory screed, one note of warmth occurs. 'God bless you, my dearest lovely girl.' Greville was attracted by her, but cautious. Mistresses cost money. He was always hard up and inclined to be close-fisted. And he was assuming responsibility for the child as well. He would hardly have done that had he had any real doubts about its paternity.

Little Emma was born and entrusted to her great-grandmother Kidd, the poor but honest and conscientious woman who had reared Emma. The regular payments from Greville were welcome, but there is sound proof that Mrs Kidd often spent more on the child than she received – a loss which was later to be made good.

With Emma as his mistress and Mrs Cadogan as a thrifty housekeeper, Greville moved to a small house in the rural and unfashionable Edgware Road.

Charles Greville was well rewarded for considering libido rather than ego. In Emma he had a young, ardent bedfellow, in Mrs Cadogan an excellent housekeeper. In an effort to economize, he left his house in Portman Square and moved to a smaller one in Edgware Road, then rural and unfashionable, and there Mrs Cadogan kept a comfortable household on £150 a year. Emma was allowed £1 a week for her personal expenses. Accounts were strictly kept, though no distinction was made, gloves jostled candles, eggs followed handkerchiefs. The coinage is now as obsolete as the noble and the groat and the prices are out of a fairy tale; a sack of coal cost three shillings and sixpence; meat for a week, five shillings and fourpence. Stockings at two shillings and tenpence were relatively expensive. One list contains an item, 'Poor man ½d', and as Sichel remarks – 'Greville must have scolded her for it, as it does not recur'.

Greville was indeed inclined to scold. There is one sad little story of one of the few outings which Emma enjoyed, a break in the rather dull routine of music lessons and drawing lessons. Greville took her to Ranelagh Gardens, then a very fashionable pleasure resort.

Ranelagh Gardens, where Emma won public applause and Greville's intense disapproval by jumping up and bursting into song.

The Gardens were tastefully laid out with flowerbeds and lawns, fountains and statues. Entertainment was provided; music, dancing, sideshows. Refreshments could be taken under shady arbours. The most respectable of women could appear there – properly escorted – and enjoy herself sedately until dusk brought a firework display. After that the fashionable world retired and the prostitutes came out in search of custom and men came in search of prostitutes.

Emma and Greville must have been there with sedate company, for what she did shocked him severely, and he made no secret of it. Some music began and Emma jumped up and sang! She loved to sing and lessons had improved her voice; her impromptu performance won applause from the crowd and that merely added to Greville's mortification. He scolded her all the way home. What he said is gone with the wind, but not difficult to imagine – unladylike, making an exhibition of herself, acting like a public performer, disgracing herself, and him. She had worn her best dress for the outing, once home she went upstairs and changed it for her very plainest. Then she knelt and wept and implored him to forgive her.

Such meekness on the part of a high-spirited girl, well aware of her talent, must be taken as the measure of her love for him. The change of dress was a sign of something else – her innate playacting streak, an eye for effect, as though no-one could be properly penitent except in penitent's garb. She related the whole story to Romney, for whom she was sitting at the time and it is believed to have inspired him to paint *The Seamstress*. (The connection is tenuous, but Romney was a genius with a genius' capacity for transmutation.)

By this time Emma must have been aware of her extraordinary beauty as well as her talent to entertain and to please and to attract men. Greville himself said later that she had received many dazzling offers. Why should she have stayed devoted to, infatuated with, Charles Greville, cold, carping and poor? One associates the word mistress with costly presents, diamonds then

(opposite) Romney painted *The Seamstress* when Emma had told him the story of herself donning penitent's garb to appease Greville after her impromptu performance at Ranelagh. This was Romney's favourite of all his portraits of Emma.

as now being a girl's best friend; Greville never gave her a worth-while trinket. Through all their association it is plain that she adored him and that he allowed himself to be adored – provided the adorer behaved well. That shrewd person who mentioned Emma's masculine streak could have been dead on the mark. She was the lover, ardent, anxious to please; Greville the mistress, cool, demanding, querulous and hard to please; an interesting reversal of roles.

In 1784 Greville's uncle, and best friend, Sir William Hamilton, came home on leave from his post as Ambassador at the Court of Naples. He was then fifty-four years old and had been a widower for two years. He was another well-connected man of small property; he had shared a wet nurse with George III and could therefore regard the King as his foster brother. He had married, in his own words, 'something against my inclination', a woman of moderate fortune, with some land in Pembrokeshire. Despite his reluctance to marry, they had lived happily and comfortably together, though she had poor health. She'd never borne a child and an adopted daughter had died.

In many ways he was like Greville, but warmer-hearted, more convivial, and with a sense of humour which Greville conspicuously lacked. He looked younger than his age, regular physical exercise had kept him in trim; he was a great walker. He tramped over the half-excavated remains of Pompeii and Herculaneum, literally picking up pieces of beauty and interest which had lain hidden under the lava and ash of the great eruption of Vesuvius in 79 AD. He was interested in Vesuvius and at least on one occasion went so near the red-hot lava that he burned his boots.

Not unexpectedly, Sir William, with his love of beautiful things, was enchanted by Emma, and she was charming to him. She called him Uncle and poured tea just to his liking; in fact he referred to her as 'the fair tea-maker of Edgware Row.' She took him into her confidence and begged him to help her in something she was planning – coaxing Greville to allow her to have Little Emma to live with them in London. Sir William saw nothing unusual or objectionable in such a scheme and courteously agreed to put in a good word at the right time.

Greville was probably in a touchy mood at the time. Between

(left) Emma at Prayer by Romney. Romney often painted Emma posed with her face upturned to disguise her small receding chin, a feature she inherited from Mrs Cadogan.

(right) Sir William Hamilton as a Knight of the Bath, nine years before he met Emma at Edgware Road in 1784. In the background of the painting there is a case of antique vases, of which he was already a famous collector. Emma's classical beauty was later to make her the prize of his collection.

uncle and nephew there had been a loose understanding – but nothing yet in legal black and white – that the younger man should be his elder's heir. Sir William was not rich by the standards of his day, but there was the property in Wales for which Greville had for some years acted as agent, and for which he had great plans. Milford Haven was to be the result. But Sir William, aged fifty-four, but looking ten years younger, might remarry,

27

(above) A plate from Sir William Hamilton's book on Greek vases.
(opposite) Many of Emma's Attitudes were inspired by paintings on Sir William's
ancient vases. The symmetry of Emma's form and features and the classical line
of her mouth reminded him of a Greek goddess.

beget a son. There were in London, and inside the complicated
family network, women of property who would be only too glad to
marry Sir William, handsome, urbane and charming. Greville
was only too glad to whisk him away to see what had been done
to develop the Welsh properties.

Meanwhile Emma was to have a holiday with her child.

The virtue of sea air and sea bathing had lately been recognized
by doctors; and although Emma enjoyed splendid health she was
prone to a rash. Nettle rash they called it. It is now sometimes
called urticaria and known to be of nervous origin, somewhat
akin to asthma.

Emma went to Hawarden to fetch the little girl, then about
two-and-a-half-years old. Mrs Kidd had spent money on Little

Emma, and one of Emma's first letters of a most revealing series, is an apology. 'My dear Greville dont be angry but I gave my granmother 5 guines for she had laid some out on her & I would not take her awhay shabbily . . . My dear Greville I wish I was with you God bless you'.

To make amends for this act of justice, which Greville might regard as extravagance, Emma chose an unfashionable holiday place and took the least expensive kind of accommodation, lodging 'in the house of a Laidy whoes husband is at sea'.

She spent the day bathing and playing with her child, and every day she wrote to Greville, adding bit to bit, a form of diary. Even at this distance in time, the letters are touching in their simplicity and trustfulness.

> Here is a great many Laidys batheing but I have no society with them as it is best not so pray my dearest Greville write soon & tell me what to do as I will do just what you think proper & tell me what to do with the child. . . . Pray my dear Greville do lett me come home as soon as you can for I am all most broken hearted being from you . . . you dont know how much I love you. . . .

Repetition would be as 'teadous' as Emma found the time away from her lover. Over and over comes the note of bereavement.

> With what impatience do I sett down to wright tell I see the postman But sure I shall have a letter to day Can you my dear Greville no you cant have forgot your poor Emma allready endead tho I am but for a few weeks absent from you my heart will not one moment leave you I am all ways thinking of you and could allmost fancy I hear you & see you.

Greville was not a good correspondent. Emma watched for the postman and knew exactly when he made his rounds.

> . . . & no letter from my dear Greville Why my dearest G – what is the reason you dont wright . . . You promised to wright before I left Hawerden . . . Pray my dear Greville, lett me go home soon I have been 3 weeks & if I stay a fortnight longer that will be 5 weeks you know . . .

Interwoven with the protestations of love, the wistful demands for letters and pleas for reunion, were mentions of the child; her physical appearance; 'she is tall good eys & brows & all to gether she will be passible'. In order to show Greville that she was not blindly besotted with her daughter Emma wrote that she was a

> guidy wild girl . . . What shall we do with her Greville . . . on satturday whe had a little quarel . . . & I did slap her on her hands & when she came to kiss me & make it up I took her on my lap & cried . . . Oh Greville you dont know how I love her endead I do when she comes & looks in my face & calls me mother endead I then truly am a mother . . .

It is no misjudgement of Greville to assume that his refusal even to consider having Little Emma to live in Edgware Road was based on the thought of what a lively romp of a child could do to his dainty house; and how much of Emma's affection and attention would be diverted from himself. When his belated letter arrived, Emma read that Greville was willing to support the child, give her a good education, but not to make her part of his household. Emma accepted his decision. 'All my happiness now is Greville & to think that he loves me . . . I have said all as I have to say abbout Emma'.

It was one of those amputations which life inflicts and it affected Emma's character. She was only nineteen and in her love for the child there may have been some element of girl-playing-with-doll, but in the main her feeling was genuinely maternal. That very natural emotion must be sealed off and forgotten – and another child was in the future to pay the price.

Little Emma went back to Hawarden. Emma had a joyful reunion with Greville, and Sir William headed South with the swallows. Outwardly nothing had changed, but that summer had seen the beginning of the end of Emma's joy in Greville. He was now firmly established as Sir William's heir and had been assured that he would have his uncle's backing if he ever needed to borrow money. With such improved prospects he could give matrimony some serious attention. He set his sight high, aiming at a lady whom he had rather feared might have caught his uncle's fancy – Lord Middleton's second daughter, better dowered than most younger sisters; she would have £30,000 when she married. It was still necessary for Greville to find a wealthy wife for the property which he would inherit would take some years to become wholly profitable.

(It is curious that this man, whom Emma adored so completely, should have failed, not only with Miss Middleton, but with every other woman to whom he offered his hand and his honourable name. His failure cannot be wholly explained by his mercenary approach – 'If I was independent I never would marry', he wrote frankly to Sir William; many marriages in the eighteenth century were made for equally sordid reasons. There must have been a flaw in the man himself, something to which Emma was blind.)

Convention demanded that a man's mistress should be out of the house before the bride moved in, and presently Greville set about the business of ridding himself of Emma – and of his responsibility for little Emma. Greville was in much the same position as any man wishing to – or compelled to – get rid of a favourite horse or dog, looking out for a good home for it. In this case what better place for Emma than in Naples with the kindly, elderly man whom she called Uncle? Such a transfer would serve another

(above) Romney's sketch of his own studio shows Greville on the far left, and Emma on the right, posing as *The Spinstress* with Romney beside her. It was in Romney's studio that Emma first developed her talent for posing that was to find its full expression in her Attitudes.

(opposite) Sir William in his study, 1777, school of Reynolds. Vesuvius in the background of the painting, the book he holds and the Etruscan vase on his left allude to his activities as volcanologist, writer and antiquarian.

purpose, too. Greville was still afraid that Sir William might yet remarry. What was left of declining sexual appetite might well be catered for by a charming young mistress.

Greville tested out the ground cautiously. He sent Sir William the picture that Romney had painted of Emma as a Bacchante – a reminder of how beautiful she was; he praised her fulsomely – not omitting to mention the part he had played in improving her character and manners. Plainly an amenable creature! And how desirable! 'I am sure she is attached to me, or she would not have refused the offers which have been great.'

It is *possible* that one offer may have come from the Prince of Wales; he was known to admire her and to have commissioned Romney to paint her; later in life he certainly sought her company and drove Nelson into a frenzy of jealousy.

The negotiations for the transfer thus tentatively begun, persisted steadily, and seem to us, in the jet age, to have taken an unconscionable time; but communications were slow: news of the Battle of Trafalgar took sixteen days to reach London. Also, Sir William had to be persuaded. He had admired Emma, declaring her to be 'better than anything in nature', and had she been a picture, a piece of statuary or an Etruscan vase his bid would have been prompt; but she was a living girl, for whose well-being and happiness he would be responsible, and he was naturally hesitant about changing his comfortable way of life. Like his nephew he was suited to a bachelor establishment, his wife, so great an invalid that her death could be regarded as 'the end of a long disease', had never been able to play much part in his social life, or shoulder the duties of an ambassadress, and he had now been alone for more than two years. Emma would disrupt his orderly household, his set ways.

Greville was obliged to be more forthright. Only necessity he wrote could force him to part with such a treasure – and then only to one he thought worthy. The happiness of his pet and her new owner was his main consideration.

(*opposite above*) Sir William with the Royal Family at Vesuvius. He once went so near the red hot lava that he burned his boots.
(*opposite below*) Sir William took great interest in the excavations of the Temple of Isis at Pompeii, where he picked up many treasures for his collection.

Greville was a devious man, but so far as his cold, complacent nature was capable of affection, he was fond of Emma, and proud of her, for he regarded her as his handiwork, something he had made out of the giddy tomboy he had met at Up Park. And it is possible that, unmanly as he was, he had a man's natural reluctance to visualize his own instrument of pleasure being used by another man. (In some places it has been customary to have discarded mistresses killed.) Greville may have imagined Sir William keeping to the avuncular role, with pretty speeches and little hand pattings. Once he actually overcame his parsimony so much as to offer to allow Emma £100 a year. Then he wrote and suggested an experimental period, 'If you could form a plan by which you could have a trial & could invite her & tell her that I ought not to leave England . . .'

It is more than likely that during his visit to England, Sir William who liked Naples, had expatiated upon its beauty and issued an invitation in a vague fashion – you must visit me some day . . .

Early in 1786 the genuine invitation was extended. Emma and her mother were to go to Naples for a six-month holiday. Circumstances made this a most feasible project; Mrs Cadogan had been ill and would benefit by the change, and Greville had business which would take him to Scotland where Emma could not accompany him. In October he would go to Naples and bring her home.

Even so, to a girl who counted absence from the beloved in days, six months was a long time, but Greville wanted her to go and her aim was to please him. She wrote and accepted the invitation. It was a humble letter, indicating that she understood that she was not to be quite on the footing of an ordinary guest – 'I shall always keep my own room when you are better engaged or go out and at other times I hope to have the pleasure of your company and conversation which will be more agreable to me than any thing in Italy'.

One reason which Greville had urged in favour of the visit was that it would improve her, and Emma was still anxious to improve. She was probably aware of her accent – she had a quick ear. She had picked up a good deal and Greville would certainly have corrected her grosser faults. She had written of Little Emma, 'she speaks countrified', very likely she knew that she did so herself at times and that she would benefit from Sir William's conversation when he had no other 'visiters'. Mrs Cadogan spoke countrified to her life's end, but Emma, unlike so many other people who have improved and scrambled up the social ladder, never disowned her. (Ouida, the famous novelist used to dress her mother as an upper servant, a kind of professional duenna.) Emma's mother was Emma's mother, while she lived Grandmother Kidd was her grandmother and her Connor cousins were her cousins. She enjoyed meeting her social superiors, and could indulge in name-dropping on occasion, but made no bones about her own humble origin. Living as she did in an age of rampant snobbery such an attitude needed more strength of character and innate assurance than it would today.

She took leave of Greville with sorrow and reluctance, but with the certainty that the separation would be of limited duration. She was blissfully ignorant of his intentions and of the protracted negotiations which had preceded her transfer.

She arrived in Naples on 16th of April 1786. It was the day she regarded as her birthday. She was twenty-one years old.

CHAPTER

2

Naples and Sir William

To live without you is impossible.

Emma to Greville

To the eye which can ignore squalor, Naples is still beautiful; in the eighteenth century, with fewer people and no industry it must have been very lovely indeed. Emma and Mrs Cadogan were straight from winter in grey London, and the pastel-coloured houses with their rust-red tiles rising tier on tier above the famous bay, the gardens in their Spring greenery, the balconies brimming with flowers, all under a sky bluer than England ever knew, must have been a visual delight, and Sir William's home, the Palazzo Sessa must have seemed like a fairy-tale place.

It was wonderfully situated, looking out across the Bay with its islands, and it was full of the beautiful things which Sir William had acquired over the years. Emma was assigned not the room she had expected, but four, all with splendid views. Sir William had set himself to soften her feeling of exile and make her happy. He knew it would be hard. On the eve of her arrival he had written to Greville, 'You may be assured that I will comfort her for the loss of you as well as I am able, but I know . . . that I shall have at times many tears to wipe from those charming eyes'.

Kindly welcomed, grandly housed, Emma sat down to write to

(previous page) The Castillo Novo at Naples by Paul Sandby; the town residence of Ferdinand IV and Maria Carolina, King and Queen of the Two Sicilies.

38

In this view of Naples, Sir William's residence, the Palazzo Sessa, is on the extreme left immediately behind the church dome.

Greville, 'it was my birthday & I was very low spirited Oh God that day that you used to smile on me & stay at home & be kind to me that that day I should be at such a distance from you – But my comfort is I rely on your promise & September or October I shall see you'.

In Naples she led a far less secluded life than she had done in London. Neapolitan society was far more easy-going – some said definitely corrupt. Everybody assumed that Emma was Sir William's mistress long before she actually became so; what other possible explanation of her presence? Nobody was critical when Sir William took her to the opera, or to the theatre. There was a colony of expatriate English in Naples, as well as a constant stream of visitors – so many that once Sir William said with humorous petulance that he wished that Magna Carta had contained a clause forbidding any English person to go abroad. Yet, though he might complain, he enjoyed his position and was capable of making it clear that anyone who snubbed Emma would not be welcome at the Embassy. There must be discrimination, of course; a young woman of Emma's dubious status could not be officially received at Court, yet the Queen of Naples and Emma met, unofficially, and liked each other long before that status was changed.

There are seven simple words, jocular, and associated with picture postcards – *Having wonderful time. Wish you were here.* They describe Emma, young, beautiful, admired, petted. She was having a wonderful time, but she was unhappy because Greville was not there to share it.

She is remembered for another love affair with a very different man, and Greville is not remembered at all, except in connection with her; but he should be remembered if only because few men have ever inspired such passionate love, and been less worthy of it.

> To live without you is imposible I love you to that degree that at this time there is not a hardship opon hearth either of poverty hunger cold death or even to walk barefooted to Scotland to see you but what I would undergo . . . I find it is not either a fine horse or a fine coach or a pack of servants – or plays or operas can make me happy it is you that as it in your power either to make me very happy or very miserable . . .

Again and again she begged him to write to her, 'pray lett me beg of you my much loved Greville onely one line from your dear dear hands.'

Adages – the summing up of human experience in a few words – have dealt with this kind of infatuation. The French say there is always one who kisses and one who allows himself to be kissed. The Spanish say that in every love affair there are two hearts, one warm, one cold; the cold one is of inestimable value, the warm one worthless, fit only to be thrown away. Emma's warm heart was thrown away. The agony of rejected love cries out in letter after letter; she must have felt the rejection when Greville failed to write. At the end of three months she wrote,

> I am now onely writing to beg of you for god sake to send me one letter if it is only a farewell . . . you have wrote one letter to me – enstead of which I have sent fourteen to you . . . I have a language

master a singing master musick &c &c, but what is it for, if it was to amuse you I should be happy – but Greville what will it avail me.

Already there were signs that Sir William's attitude toward her had ceased to be Platonic – if indeed it had ever been wholly so. He was an experienced diplomat and took his time; he was a kindly man and saw that any suggestion of a change in their relationship must imply a total break with Greville. He wooed her indirectly by indulging her and trying to keep her amused.

Later on people who disliked or envied her were to call her coarse, yet two of her references to Sir William's approaches show the utmost delicacy.

> I have had a conversation this morning with Sr Wm that has made me mad he speaks half I do not know what to make of it. [And again] I have lived with you 5 years & you have sent me to a strange place & no one prospect me thinking you was coming to me, instead of which I was told . . . no I respect him but no never . . . I tell you give me one guiney a week for every thing & live with me & I will be contented.

She did her best to show Greville how highly other people valued her; Lord Hervey was her slave, a foreign prince was enamoured, the King had raised his hat to her; Angelica Kauffman was painting her and all the ladies of Naples were trying, by artificial means, to match her complexion.

For Greville the affair had ended when Emma set out for Naples, and what could such letters rouse in him but a cold distaste? Yet he preserved them whereas Nelson, in love to the end, destroyed her letters as soon as he had read and reread them. Perhaps the outpourings, unwelcome though they might be at the moment, appealed to the Narcissus streak in Greville, flattering his self-image.

At last he wrote, sending her a present, a blue hat and gloves as a palliative to soften the blow. 'Oblige Sir William', he wrote.

She replied, beginning with red-hot rage that dwindled down to pathos.

> Greville to advise me, you that used to envy my smiles now with cooll indifference to advise me . . . if I was with you I would murder you & myself boath . . . nothing shall ever do for me but going home to you – if that is not to be I will except of nothing I will go to London their go in to every excess of vice tell I dye a miserable broken hearted wretch & leave my fate as a warning to young whomin never to be

two good, for now you have made me love you you made me good you have abbandoned me & some violent end shall finish our connexion if it is to finish, but oh Greville you cannot you must not give me up, you have not the heart to do it . . . I allways knew I have ever had a forebodeing – since I first begun to love you – that I was not destined to be happy for their is not a king or prince on hearth that could make me happy without you . . .

Then, after expressing envy of the paper he had handled, and the wafer which sealed it, since it had touched his lips, she ends, 'pray write as often as you can . . . & if you come we shall all go home together . . . Pray write to me & dont write in the stile of a freind but a lover for I wont hear a word of freind . . . Sir William is our freind, but we are lovers. I am glad you have sent me a blue hat & gloves. . .'

Sir William had foreseen many tears and Mrs Cadogan, who knew Emma better than anyone else could do, must have had forebodings, too. While Emma was accepting the inevitable, their lot was unenviable; tears and temper alternated and the Emma who emerged from this shattering experience was changed. The word *traumatic* is relatively modern, and slightly anachronistic here, but it merely means produced by wounds and Emma had been wounded to the heart and in a way that less wholehearted, one-track-minded people could never know. Something had been lost forever.

Goethe greatly admired her, for her beauty, for her skill in portraying any character, any emotion, with no more apparatus than two shawls and a handkerchief, but he said a very cogent thing about her as a person. She lacked soul. Another, less famous admirer remarked that perhaps Miss Hart was no more than a living image. Both were right. What Sir William inherited from his nephew was not quite what that nephew had enjoyed, but it suited him, and Emma was a consummate actress and could doubtless give as good a performance between the sheets as on a stage with two shawls. And Nature's abhorrence of a vacuum played its part; ambition and the desire for self-advancement crept in.

(opposite) Emma's favourite representation of herself was as the Comic Muse, painted by Angelica Kauffmann, the foremost artist in Naples.

Emma's Attitudes soon became famous
in Naples. The spectator 'sees what thousands
of artists would have liked to express,
realised before him in movements
and surprising transformations – one pose
follows another without a break. She knows how
to arrange the folds of her veil to
match each mood, and has a hundred ways of
turning it into a headdress.' *Goethe*

44

She still wrote to Greville – the habit was hard to break, and she wanted him to know how well she was managing without him. One day she wrote, 'Pray write . . . it is not to your intrest to disoblidge me for you dont know the power I have hear . . . if you affront me I will make him marry me'. Greville dismissed that as an idle threat; few men married their mistresses, why buy what one already possessed? And in fact it took Emma all her charm and tact and talent to achieve her aim.

Sir William had his position to consider. And his career. It was one thing for the English Ambassador to a distant, and not very highly considered country to keep a young, beautiful, talented mistress; to take her as his wife was another. When next he returned to England could he expect George III and his strictly conventional Queen to acknowledge a woman of low birth and bad reputation? Could he even be sure of the King and Queen of Naples? Neither of them had a spotless sexual record and their Court was not renowned for high moral standards, but a facade of respectability must be preserved. They might like and admire Emma in her present capacity, but they might resent having her thrust upon them as the wife of the British Ambassador.

Also, Sir William would have been less than human if he had not regarded the present position as very comfortable; during the day when he was busy with his official duties, or shooting and boar-hunting with the King, or following his antiquarian interests, Emma was taking lessons or being painted. When he came home she was there. If, after a hunting trip he were chilled, she brewed him rum punch. She entertained his guests with her Attitudes. She was still anxious to please. Why change what was so good for something which might be less so?

What exactly went on in the Palazzo Sessa, when they were alone, nobody now can know. Greville, commending her to Sir William had written that she had not a grain of avarice or self-interest and that her only fault was an unequal temper – 'I never was irritated by her momentary passions'. How many momentary passions did Sir William suffer and ignore? And how far was Emma's ambition buoyed up by the many tributes paid to her beauty? In distant Russia the wicked old Empress, Catherine the Great, heard through envoys rumours of the exceptional loveliness of the English girl in Naples and demanded a portrait of her. Cameo cutters were busy carving her profile. Simple people in Naples half-identified her with the Virgin Mary. As she wrote to Greville, 'Last night there was two preists come to our house & Sir William made me put the shawl over my head & look up and the preist burst in to tears & kist my feet & said God had sent me a purpose'.

Cameo cutters of Naples used Emma's
profile as a model.

Short of making her the proposal upon which she had set her heart, Sir William did everything he could to please her; he had the wall opposite the window of one of her rooms lined with mirrors, so that she saw the wonderful view whichever way she looked. He built a music room where she could sing and give her performances; he introduced her to the most well-born English visitors, such as the Duchess of Argyll who promptly became her friend, thus making lesser ladies who had been coolly civil to do some rethinking. The Duchess, who by her first marriage had become the Duchess of Hamilton and thus related to Sir William, may have given him some kinswomanly advice. Emma was presently so acceptable everywhere – except at Court – that it was rumoured that she was already married to Sir William.

She was now at the very peak of her beauty and must have had many offers from men who were younger, richer, more illustrious than Sir William yet her behaviour was faultless. In a society to which scandal was meat and drink, no breath of it ever touched her.

Sir William may have let fall some word about his fear of Court reaction; if he did not she had sense enough to guess what

The English Garden at Caserta was designed by Sir William Hamilton. It was here that King Ferdinand made his advances to Emma – an incident that resulted in Maria Carolina approving her as a suitable wife for Sir William.

was impeding him, and she took action of a kind which foretold the gambler she was later to become.

Adjoining the Palazzo Sessa and lying between it and the Royal Palace was an expanse known as the English Garden. It was a fad, just as Italian gardens had for years been a fad in England. An English garden was informal, made to resemble – often by highly artificial means – the wildness of Nature. Emma, properly attended, was walking there one afternoon when she was accosted by a man whom she recognized as the King. She knew him well by sight, and knew that he admired her. Quite early during her stay in Naples he had expressed his regret that he did not speak

English; and when he had heard her sing he paid her the highest compliment he could, she sang, he said, like a king, meaning himself, he considered himself a splendid vocalist.

Language was no longer a barrier, Emma had acquired Italian quickly and easily. She rebuffed the accoster, but he knew that had the snub been seriously intended, she would have gone, with the attendant, back to the Palazzo Sessa; as it was she walked on towards one of those secluded places which were a characteristic of an English garden; King Ferdinand tipped the attendant who disappeared. The King then made the kind of proposition likely to tempt a woman of easy virtue. Emma said that she could not begin to consider such an offer until it was set down in writing. So Ferdinand wrote.

On what, with what, one asks oneself. History can be maddeningly silent about such details. Bent on seduction and accustomed

Ferdinand IV of Naples had little education
apart from in the field sports of the day.
He gladly handed over the reins of
government to his wife, Maria Carolina,
leaving himself free to pursue a bucolic
and amatory existence.

to the service of secretaries, Ferdinand was unlikely to have
come armed with writing implements. Emma – and the whole
thing seems to be the result of careful planning, may have carried
sketching materials, or some of those little ivory tablets and a
pencil. When the promises were in writing, Emma fobbed the
King off, and went straight to the Queen, sure of admittance,
though not officially received. She then gave Queen Maria
Carolina a display of histrionics; she knelt and wept and begged
the Queen to use her influence to shield her from such unsolicited
attentions, otherwise she would have no alternative but to seek
refuge in a convent. Maria Carolina asked who had pestered
Emma; Emma did not know, but she produced the writing which
the Queen recognized.

Maria Carolina was not shocked by this evidence of proposed
infidelity. She and her husband, while producing a sizable family,
had been tolerant of each other's extramarital adventures,
providing some discretion were exercised. In trying to seduce
Emma, Ferdinand had not been discreet. The last thing Maria
Carolina wanted was to offend the British Ambassador, well-
known to dote upon his lovely mistress. And such a move as the
King was contemplating could not possibly be made quietly;
Emma was too well-known, her beauty was famous.

The Queen of Naples was not invariably successful in her
diplomacy, but she had some skill, the veiled hint, the roundabout approach, the unfinished sentence. It was easy for her, once
she had decided that Emma, though likeable, was potentially
dangerous, to send for Sir William and indicate that as Lady
Hamilton she would be welcome at the Court of Naples – or, as it

was sometimes called, the Court of the Two Sicilies. And Sir William was not the man to need things spelt out to him in large letters. He understood that his marriage to Emma would be acceptable in Naples; why not in England?

Politics are almost invariably boring; geography and history can be – served up in cold slabs, but for the understanding of Emma's story some light background sketches are needed.

Italy, in Emma's day – and until its unification – was merely a geographical term for a piece of land divided between several large states and more smaller ones, always rivals, sometimes active enemies, incapable, even under threat from outside of any real cooperation. In most cases the name of the principal city applied to as much of the surrounding countryside as the city could control. Naples was a city, Naples was also a state, one of the largest, extending a third of the way up the 'leg' of Italy, and in the eighteenth century including the island of Sicily. This was the Kingdom of the Two Sicilies, though Neapolitans hated and despised the Sicilians and the Sicilians felt the same way about the Neapolitans.

The area – mainland and island, had always been a target for ambitious men, since classical times; it dominated the Mediterranean and was – with the exception of Gibraltar, the nearest Europe came to Africa. The Normans had established a kingdom there years before the Conquest of England was contemplated. France and Spain had competed for its possession. In Emma's day it was, though independent, regarded as the natural heritage of younger sons of the Spanish Royal Family. Ferdinand, the second son of the King of Spain, had inherited the Two Sicilies when he was eight years old and when he was seventeen married Maria Carolina, the eldest daughter of the great Maria Theresa of Austria, and sister to Marie Antoinette.

Maria Theresa had reared her daughters to rule, autocratically but well and then married them to inherently stupid men. (Marie Antoinette's husband, Louis XVI of France, wrote 'Rien' in his diary for the day when the sacking of the Bastille ushered in the Revolution.) Marie Antoinette took refuge in frivolity, mainly harmless, Maria Carolina turned to government. Ferdinand was glad to hand over responsibility to her, and to be free to go hunting, drinking, whoring. Maria Carolina took her job seriously and brought about several reforms for which people – especially the poor – should have been grateful; she freed the roads of tolls, encouraged agriculture and industry, supported education – even for women – and was a patron of the arts. Somehow she missed popularity except with the tiny minority of intellectuals, whereas Ferdinand was extremely popular at both extremes of the social scale; with the nobility who were generally ill-educated, coarse-mannered and not far removed from the robber barons who had been their forebears; with the riffraff of the streets. With his nobles Ferdinand could indulge in field sports and practical jokes – often brutal. He could eat and drink to excess and generally behave as though he were one of them. He liked to go among the poor, sometimes as himself, sometimes lightly disguised, and share their holidays, pastimes and religious festivals.

In 1791, Sir William was due for leave. Emma told everyone that he intended to ask King George to give his approval to their marriage. That was exactly what happened. Sir William was granted the audience usual for all returning Ambassadors, at it mentioned his request and was given the King's grudging consent.

George III was understandably touchy about mistresses. As a young man he had loved Hannah Lightfoot, a Quakeress, and had a child by her; that association had been broken up by family pressure and he had then set his heart on a lady of rank. To prevent further misbehaviour his marriage was arranged; a portrait of his wife is proof that Victorianism did not begin with Victoria. George's envy of any man who enjoyed an illicit love affair may have been unconscious but it resulted in a stern disapproval which extended to his sons when they took mistresses, and here was a man of rank, sixty-one years of age who having enjoyed a pretty young mistress for a long time, was now about to marry her! One thing was certain, Emma would never be received at Court; and though no-one then could have guessed it, the King's disapproval was to have an effect on other lives than Emma's.

(opposite) George III, King of England, by Allan Ramsay. The Court in England was far more formal than the Court in Naples. It was only grudgingly that George III consented to Sir William's marriage with Emma, when they returned to England in 1791.

Sir William's family took on the whole a more lenient view and the engaged couple were lavishly entertained; and Emma herself gave performances. At Richmond the Duke of Queensberry organized a concert centring upon her singing and her Attitudes; at William Beckford's still unfinished Gothic Structure of Fonthill Abbey, her acting moved a very sophisticated audience to tears. Romney took a paternal pride in her and may have been prejudiced when he said that her acting surpassed anything he had ever seen, it 'is simple, grand, terrible and pathetic', but Horace Walpole, a practising cynic admired her too. An experienced impresario offered her a contract – £2,000 a year and the proceeds of two benefit concerts. Notoriety may have been part of the attraction – but it was only a nine days' wonder, without talent to back it the man would have been making a bad bargain.

Sir William and Emma went to see Jane Powell perform at Drury Lane and afterwards went backstage where the two former maids of Dr Budd greeted each other with affection and mutual, if tacit, congratulations. Such a contact with the humble past, made voluntarily, was further proof of Emma's lack of pretentiousness. She told Romney that she was anxious to be 'the same Emma', but the artist's eye noticed and his hand set down for posterity, a sometimes incongruous sadness about the eyes; the wound which Greville had inflicted had left its mark.

How Greville felt about the engagement is unrecorded, which is a pity because he must have felt something – even if only a regret that his inheritance was endangered, and that danger brought about by the very measures he had taken to protect it. Whatever his feelings, he contrived to remain on the best of terms with his uncle and the woman who would be his aunt. Did he ever remember; 'but we was lovers'?

Amid all the gaiety of that summer, Emma made time to visit Hawarden, where Little Emma lived with her great-grandmother when not at school in Manchester, where the fees were costing Sir William £100 a year, a fairly substantial sum to pay for a girl's education.

The wedding took place at Marylebone Church, which had long associations with the Hamilton family, and also had the distinction of being the smallest church serving the largest parish in London. It was so small that it had no font and baptisms were

The well-known actress Jane Powell, who was once
a maid at Dr Budd's with Emma.

made from a bowl on the altar. It was a very quiet wedding,
witnessed by Lord Abercorn, a relative of Sir William's and a
friend from the Diplomatic Service. That Emma recognized the
legal importance of the day is shown by her signature in the
register – Emily Lyon, her genuine name.

She was not in love with Sir William, but she was deeply
grateful; he had made a respectable woman of her and she told
Romney that she could never repay him for restoring her to
innocence and happiness. The wedding day must have been a
happy day for Mrs Cadogan, too. Judged by some strict moral
standards her conduct had not been wholly admirable, too
tolerant, too conniving, but she had little choice. Had she taken
a critical, holier-than-thou attitude she would have lost Emma;
as it was they enjoyed a relationship that both valued. Mrs
Cadogan knew the world for what it was, a hard place for the

poor; one must make the best of what offered, and do the best one could in any situation. From the little we know directly of her, a few remarks, a few letters, she seems to have been a woman of sound good sense, capable of keeping her head in a crisis. She also lacked pretentiousness and the change from being the over-complaisant mother of a kept woman to being Sir William's mother-in-law seems to have affected her not at all. She still dressed as a housekeeper, still kept check on household bills, and it is significant that Emma's most acute financial crises occurred after her death.

Even as a decently married woman, Emma was not received at the English Court. This may have affronted Sir William more than it did Emma, for he left England gladly that autumn and said that he intended to spend the remainder of his life in Naples.

In 1791 the French Revolution was two years old, but England and France were at peace; there were a good number of people in England who wholeheartedly approved of the Revolution, thinking it long overdue. The bloodiest time, known as the Reign of Terror was still to come and there was hope that a constitutional government, something like that of England might be set up, with Louis XVI at its head. But in June 1791, while Emma and Sir William were enjoying the hospitality of great country houses, Louis and Marie Antoinette had made an inept attempt to escape from France, and, brought back, subjected to a more rigorous form of 'house arrest' than they suffered before. But Marie Antoinette was allowed a visit from His Britannic Majesty's Ambassador to Naples. Marie Antoinette seized upon this opportunity to communicate with Maria Carolina. Emma always said that she carried the doomed Queen's last *letter* to her sister. The statement has been questioned; was it a letter, or a verbal message? Was it actually the last? Many of Emma's statements and claims have been similarly questioned; she overexaggerated, she dramatized, but when everything she claimed had been most carefully sieved, usually the true grain of truth remained. What she took back to Naples may well have been Marie Antoinette's last letter to her sister.

Not that there was anything to hope for from Naples. It was too far away, its army was an ill-officered rabble, and in order to maintain any kind of navy at all Maria Carolina had been obliged to appoint an Englishman, Sir John Acton, as Admiral. A little later, when Naples was at war and its army had been defeated in a battle, Nelson said, 'The Neapolitan officers have not lost much honour, for God knows they had but little to lose; but they have lost all they had.' And even Acton failed to weld the Neapolitan Navy into a useful fighting force.

Sir John Acton.

Marie Antoinette would have been unlikely to ask for help from her sister; she put more faith in Austria, her native land, and in the army of émigrés who had escaped in time and was now mustering beyond the Rhine, both held in check by the French Government's threat that any attack would be fatal for the King and Queen. So the message Emma carried was unlikely to have been of political significance.

Almost from the moment of its delivery, Lady Hamilton became the close friend and confidante of the Queen of Naples. It is not unusual for people isolated by high position to develop a reliance upon and a fondness for, somebody outside their immediate circle, somebody trustworthy, somebody upon whom to unload their anxieties and worries. Maria Carolina had many worries at the time. She hated what had happened in France, dreaded what might happen to her sister. She knew that anarchy was contagious and that Naples had no guard against it. Even Spain, ruled by Ferdinand's brother was a potential enemy, for his wife greatly coveted the Two Sicilies for her own second son and in order to get it would ally with France no matter who might rule there.

In such circumstances, Emma was the perfect friend, sympathetic, yet at the same time capable of adopting an attitude of confidence and optimism and she was not handicapped by holding an official position. She was passionately patriotic and although there is no record of her ever saying it, it is almost sure that she assured Maria Carolina that the English would never allow what had happened in Paris to happen in Naples. Look at the map! Would England ever allow the French to dominate the Mediterranean, one of the gateways to India?

Maria Carolina found Emma far easier to talk to than Sir William who could only say what he was authorized to say, and who seemed to ignore the gravity of the situation. Although he liked Naples, he had a poor opinion of Neapolitans as a whole and wrote that 'provided they can get their bellies full at a cheap rate', they would not bother about what was happening in other countries. Also, during this tense time, with spies everywhere, it was inadvisable for the British Ambassador to appear to be on very close terms with the Queen of Naples. Emma was free to come and go, just a woman, a pretty woman who knew nothing of politics. In some quarters quite another construction was placed upon Emma's intimacy with the Queen.

Marie Antoinette's enemies had not hesitated to accuse her of such ill-assorted vices as immorality with men, Lesbianism with her friend, the Princesse de Lamballe, and incest with her own young son. A similar element in Naples held that the relationship between the Queen and Emma was an unnatural one. If this *canard* ever reached Emma's ears she would have laughed heartily. It may have been her uninhibited laugh, her language when in a temper, which made her critics say that she lacked refinement. Long after she was dead the belief still held – not unbased – well-bred people smiled often but seldom laughed noisily, others laughed heartily but were sparing with their smiles.

In January 1793, Louis XVI of France went to the guillotine, accused of conspiring against the national safety; his Queen and his sister, after a time of the utmost humiliation, followed him, and soon England and France were at war, not because regicide and nameless atrocities had been committed but because France had declared her intention of converting the people of other nations to revolution and a spurious egalitarianism, if necessary by force of arms.

With the declaration of war, two threads of destiny, emerging from very remote beginnings, drew closer, following courses bound to impinge.

CHAPTER

3

Nelson

The British Fleet under my command
could never have returned a second
time to Egypt had not Lady Hamilton's
influence with the Queen of Naples
caused letters to be wrote . . .

Nelson's Codicil

Horatio Nelson was born in September 1758, at the Rectory of
Burnham Thorpe in Norfolk. (It is worth noting how many
people who achieve eminence, have a similar background:
Cecil Rhodes, the Brontes, Edith Cavell, Sir Laurence Olivier, to
make a haphazard selection.) His mother was connected on one
side of her family with the Walpole's, many of them titled, but
although the first Baron Walpole acted as godfather to one of
Horatio's brothers who died young, and the second Baron under-
took the same duties for Nelson, ties were not close and it seems
that the Nelsons did not look to the Walpoles for any material
benefits – a sub-branch of the family, the Sucklings, were to prove
far more useful.

Nelson's mother died when he was nine years old; she was
forty-two and had had eleven children in seventeen years. Eight
survived her to be brought up by their father who, though un-
worldy, was strict. They were poor and lived frugally. One Suckling uncle with a secure post in the Customs and Excise, found an
opening for Maurice, the eldest son, and another, Captain

(previous page) The start of Nelson's great victory at Aboukir Bay, *The Battle of
the Nile*, painted by Nicholas Pocock. Captain Foley surprised the French line
by sailing the *Goliath* round to attack from the landward side.

Nelson was born at the Rectory of Burnham Thorpe in September 1798. This painting by F. Pocock shows Nelson carrying a flag in the foreground.

Suckling, took Nelson to sea with him, at the age of twelve. His letter, in reply to a request to do so, was blunt. 'What has poor little Horatio done that he should be sent to rough it at sea? But let him come, and if a cannon ball takes off his head he will at least be provided for.'

Not an auspicious beginning, but the fair, frail-looking boy survived, eager to learn, quite fearless, dedicated to his job. A seasick cabin boy at twelve, at fourteen a member of a Polar expedition, experience in the East Indies; at eighteen judged to be

At the age of fourteen, Nelson went on an unsuccessful Arctic expedition to find the Northeast Passage. His attempt to acquire a polar bear skin for his father also failed when his musket misfired, and he was only saved from an early death by a signal shot from his ship, which scared the bear off.

capable of commanding a ship, and at twenty-two he held the rank of post-captain. That was rapid promotion for a young man with no influence behind him, but England was at war with her rebellious American colonies, and as Nelson wrote to his father, 'We all rise by deaths. I got my rank by a shot killing a post-captain.' He added that he hoped to die in action.

He almost died of disease when he was sent to the Caribbean to enforce the Navigation Acts – seeing that no American ship traded with England's most precious Sugar Islands. The climate and the various fevers, notably malaria and Yellow Jack, killed soldiers and sailors by the thousand every year. Once again Nelson, though extremely ill, survived, and at the age of twenty-eight married a young widow, Frances – Fanny Nisbet. It is unlikely that she married him for his looks; a description of him at the time curiously resembles that of the young Napoleon, lank-haired, shabby, ill-groomed; unimpressive at first sight, but – and again like Napoleon – get him into conversation, especially on professional matters and a mysterious inner fire glowed. He was not yet famous, but Prince William, the King's son who was serving his time with the Fleet, thought highly enough of Nelson to act as his best man at the little white church at St Nevis. Fanny, radiant in lace, was certain of Nelson's love, certain that he would make a good husband and a good stepfather to her son, Josiah, then aged nine. And eleven years later, after his great victory at the Battle of the Nile when Nelson was asked if this were not the happiest day of his life, he replied that it was not; his happiest day was the one on which he had married his wife.

People overanxious to serve Emma and exonerate Nelson have tried to depict Fanny as a cold hard woman, and the marriage as a failure. The truth was otherwise. Fanny endeared herself to all Nelson's family, especially to his father who became, and remained much attached to her. The only thing to be regretted was that she did not give Nelson, who was fond of children, a child of his own. He did his best with his stepson, not a very satisfactory boy.

The war ended and there was the inevitable call for disarmament and economy; ships were laid up, soldiers and sailors begged in the streets. Nelson and Fanny were more fortunate than most; he had his half-pay and she had the income from her £4,000, a dowry from her uncle. They had no home, but were welcome at Burnham Thorpe where the Reverend Edmund Nelson was so anxious that they should feel that the house was their own that he spent long periods lodging in his two subsidiary parishes. Nelson had a brother, Rector of Hilborough and two sisters within easy reach. Fanny had her father-in-law's garden, which he had tended carefully, planting lilac and syringa and hyacinths and roses, and Nelson farmed the ten acre glebe which by law had been part of every country living from time immemorial. But he was a dedicated sailor, 'on the beach', and it was a period of frustration for him. He could have been difficult to live with, but he was fundamentally a man of good nature, well schooled in self-discipline.

As soon as the war broke out between England and France, he appealed to the Admiralty, begging to be given command of something, 'though it were only a cockle boat'. He was given a second-class battleship and sent to join the Mediterranean Fleet whose chief duty was to keep the French ships bottled up in the ports of Southern France. It was boring work and until the

French would come out and fight, there could be no hope of prize money, a thing which all sailors, except those with independent means, largely depended, since their pay was so miserly. Nelson did manage out of his, however, to send his father £200, an act typical of the generosity which – combined with bad luck – was to keep him poor all his life.

He saw some action, and was wounded during this time. He took part in the siege of Corsica, then a French island, and was hit, not by a bullet but a spurt of gravel which partially destroyed the sight of his right eye, without disfiguring it in any way. He was not so blind on that side as popular legend holds, for later on, when his left eye was overstrained he wore a green shield over it and managed with what sight was left in the injured one.

Meanwhile, with Napoleon in charge, the French Army was everywhere victorious; the Austrians were driven out of Northern Italy and the conquerors were hailed by the common people as liberators. The war was advancing towards Naples; and as Maria Carolina had feared, Spain had become the ally of France.

Emma was one of the first people to know that Spain intended to do so. Ferdinand had a secret letter from his brother, the King of Spain, and showed it to his wife, who told Emma about it and even allowed her to make a copy of it. Sir William transmitted the bad news, in cypher, to London. This service to her country has been questioned, but the truth was vouched for by Sir William, just as her later services were vouched for by Nelson.

Looking back on her, in the last of the pre-Nelson days, one is amazed by the sheer scope of her activities. She was the support and confidante of Maria Carolina who, but for her training would have given way to hysteria: she was the leader of Neapolitan society, which was frenziedly gay, and she was nursing Sir William through his first serious illness. For eight days she did not remove her clothes, and hardly ate anything. Yet in the midst of it all she had a thought to spare for her grandmother Kidd. She wrote to Greville – a natural thing to do, since he was still acting as agent for Sir William's property in Wales. She did not address him as her dearest Greville, but as Mr Greville.

You must know I send my grandmother every Cristmas twenty pounds & so I ought. I have 2 hundred a year for nonsense & it wou'd be hard I cou'd not give her twenty pounds when she as so often given me her last shilling. As Sir Wm is ill I cannot ask him for the order but if you will get the twenty pounds & send it to her you will do me the greatest favour for if the time passes without hearing from me she may imagine I have forgot her & I wou'd not keep her poor old heart in suspense for the world . . . the fourth of November last I had a dress on that cost twenty five pounds as it was gala at Court & believe me I felt unhappy all the while I had it on.

As much as – more than – any letter she ever wrote, this reveals the true Emma as she was before life took another misshapening twist. The mention of the expensive dress is in direct contradiction with her later attitude towards money; her consideration for the feelings of an old woman, far away in Wales shows a lively imagination.

She wore that expensive dress at a Gala, for Naples, enjoying a shaky neutrality, was trying to keep up its morale and to divert public attention from the presence of the omnipotent French troops in the Papal States on her Northern border. Maria Carolina had done what she could; she had asked people to send their French servants home; she had issued a decree that made any gathering of more than ten people illegal; a few obviously Jacobin sympathisers were gaoled; and there was an agreement that no Neapolitan or Sicilian port should harbour more than four foreign ships – other than French – at one time.

Austria was defeated, Prussia had withdrawn, Spain had joined France and England was virtually alone and threatened with invasion, the Mediterranean Fleet was recalled to defend its homeland. Nelson went to join Admiral Sir John Jervis who was watching for the Spanish Fleet, which was moving to join the French at Brest. The Battle of St Vincent was fought on St Valentine's Day, 1797. It was a great victory in which Nelson highly distinguished himself. Sir John Jervis was given an earldom, and Nelson was created a Knight of the Bath. It is sad to think that for years after – though remaining on amicable personal terms, they were fighting a legal battle about the distribution of the prize money.

Fanny, later to be accused of not appreciating him, wrote very warmly, at the same time begging him not to undertake unnecessary risks. 'I sincerely hope, my dear husband, that all these

(left) Admiral Sir John Jervis was created Earl St Vincent after he won the Battle of St Vincent on St Valentine's Day, 1797. Nelson distinguished himself highly, and was created Knight of the Bath.

(right) The arms and supporters of Rear Admiral Sir Horatio Nelson, K.B., Nelson's official title after he was knighted.

wonderful and daring actions – such as boarding ships – you will leave to others . . . you have acquired a character or name which, all hands agree, cannot be greater, therefore, rest satisfied.'

Of such wifely instructions he took no notice and in the summer was sent with a hopelessly inadequate force to storm Teneriffe, where a fleet of treasure ships from Mexico were supposed to be in harbour. In that unsuccessful engagement his right arm was so shattered that it had to be amputated, and for nine months after that he was convalescent, cared for by Fanny. This time he was sure that his career was ended and that he was beached for life. Who would want a sailor with a partially blind eye and only one arm?

England did.

By 1798, Napoleon, having proved himself invincible on land was planning an enterprise which at least in its initial stage would involve ships. He intended to use Egypt as a jumping off place for the conquest of India. Rumours reached England of men and ships mustering in the ports of Southern France and in French held Italian ports. The secret of their destination was well-kept, and when Nelson returned to the Mediterranean in May 1798 he had no precise orders save to find and intercept and to prevent at all costs, the French Fleet slipping away into the Atlantic.

On a map of the world the Mediterranean looks small, but it is over two-thousand-miles long and in places five-hundred-miles wide, a big hunting ground. Nelson had no swift frigates to go scouting. After more than a month of abortive hunting, with water low in the casks and a great dearth of the fresh food which kept the dreaded scurvy at bay. Nelson sought shelter and supplies at the Sicilian port of Syracuse. The governor refused to allow entry. He was holding to the rules which had allowed Naples alone of the states in Italy to retain even a show of independence; but Emma, pressing hard on the Queen, got the ships rewatered and revictualled. Nelson wanted more, through Sir William he begged the King and Queen of Naples to come out into the open against the French; to lend him frigates and gunboats and help strike a blow which would free not only Naples but Europe. He knew now where the French were – making for Alexandria – and he knew that in a sea battle he could defeat them.

He did not get what he asked for, properly, through Sir William; Emma got what she asked for; and Nelson went on and won the Battle of the Nile. It was another spectacular victory, and it brought him another wound; possibly one to which not quite enough attention has been paid. A piece of metal hit him on the head, violently enough to dislodge a flap of flesh from his forehead, which fell forward and made him temporarily completely blind. It was put back, in the rough and ready way of the day, but it left him with a new affliction – severe headaches; what else did it leave? Nowadays medical science knows a little more about what a severe blow on the head can do to the brain, how dangerously interdependent body and mind are. Nelson's genius was not impaired; nobody noticed any change in his nature or character, but his subsequent behaviour strongly suggests that something had gone slightly off course.

Love at first sight is in the high romantic tradition, but when Nelson came back to Naples and Emma greeted him, crying, 'O God! Is it possible?' and fell in a swoon, it was not their first meeting. During his earlier service in the Mediterranean, Nelson

(above) A cartoon of the Battle of the Nile showing Nelson chaining up the French fleet and beating them with 'British Oak'.
(opposite) The liaison between Emma and Nelson began in a whirl of festivities to celebrate his victory at the Nile, and what was believed to be the end of French domination in Europe.

had visited Naples and been entertained at the Embassy. He had mentioned Lady Hamilton in a letter to Fanny, in the most ordinary way, just as he might have mentioned any other woman. From then on he had maintained a desultory correspondence with Sir William, whom he liked and respected, who liked and admired him. During the negotiations about rewatering and revictualling the Fleet, Nelson had written to Emma, a cool, querulous letter, beginning; 'My dear Madam'. In September he would be forty years old; Emma had kept her thirty-third birthday in the April of that year, so the feeling that sprang up between them could hardly be attributed to youth; or to inexperience. Before settling upon Fanny, Nelson had been greatly attracted to two or three other women; Emma had loved Greville wholeheartedly, and felt for Sir William a great affection and gratitude.

Nelson was a man of very strong religious conviction and of the highest possible honour; the man who, badly wounded, insisted upon taking his turn, no priority, in the bloody cockpit where the

surgeons worked; the man who, under the nose of two enemy ships, halted his in order to pick up one of his crew who had fallen overboard. In theory it was inconceivable that such a man should even contemplate cuckolding his friend, his host, under his own roof. His giving way to infatuation was completely out of character. So, in a way, was Emma's; the spotless garment of Holy Matrimony had, thanks to Sir William, been spread over her dubious past, she enjoyed being respectable and respected; she would surely have been one of the last women in the world to invite any further scandal. Yet both of them, with sound reasons for not doing so, fell in love and gave the world not only one of its most remarkable but one of its most tragic stories.

It is not only possible, but likely, that had Nelson and the ships under his command been immediately withdrawn to cooler waters and a different climate, Emma Hamilton would have sunk back into Nelson's memory – a beautiful woman who had done the Fleet a good service and whom he had repaid in a fashion, by bringing back from Egypt a present for her, a young Nubian girl, called Fatima.

Earlier in the century a dark-skinned attendant – more usually boy than girl – had been part of a fashionable lady's outfit. Technically such children were slaves – a silver collar engraved with the owner's name was quite common – but while they stayed small they were generally treated as pets, more indulged, extravagantly dressed. When they had outgrown their decorative role they found more menial work. But in 1774 Lord Mansfield, somewhat against his will, gave judgment in a case concerning a runaway slave, no slave could exist in England. With that the fashion began to dwindle and Nelson's gift to Emma was slightly old-fashioned.

The liaison between Emma and Nelson began in a whirl of festivities to celebrate his victory and the belief, which was premature, that this was the end of French domination. No city in the world at the time was better able to stage balls and banquets, concerts and receptions than Naples, no people in the world readier to seize upon an excuse for merrymaking. Sir William had once noted that everyone who came to Naples seemed to undergo a change; to become slightly mad. Nelson, not fully recovered from his head wound was the hero of the hour, Emma the heroine. He hated the whole procedure as much as she enjoyed it. Nelson wrote to Lord St Vincent that Naples was a country of fiddlers, puppets and scoundrels. 'No place for a simple sailor', and that he must keep clear of it. But his flagship was damaged and he could not get away after four days, as he had intended, and before he could get away he was bewitched. 'The Conqueror is become the Conquered', he wrote to her later.

Sir William's attitude was, and remains baffling. One thinks; He must have known! One thinks; He could not have known and remained Nelson's friend! One thinks; He knew, understood and

(opposite) Emma as *The Ambassadress,* by Romney, was completed on the day of her marriage to Sir William in September 1791, on her return from Marylebone Church. The ever-present Vesuvius is behind her, and she wears one of her favourite blue velvet hats.

(overleaf) *Nelson and Emma at Posillipo* painted by Serres in 1798. Nelson would have visited Emma at the 'Villa Emma' at Posillipo, while refitting the damaged British Fleet at the shipyards there.

decided to be tolerant. He was not a man to take his emotional temperature every hour and record it, so one can only guess.

Naturally no man is anxious to clap the horns on his own head; no man of chivalry is anxious to besmirch the reputation of the woman of whom he is fond. Sir William was a gentleman of what even then was recognized as the old school; he had his dignity to consider. And perhaps his well-being. He was sixty-eight and his health was beginning to fail. Emma had been his young, beautiful mistress, his young, impeccably behaved wife, his devoted nurse. Inside the bed she was probably of no value to him; outside it she was irreplaceable.

There was, of course the Press, with snide remarks, cruel cartoons, enjoying a freedom undreamed of in today's permissive society. One paper went too far and told an ugly story about the hero of the Nile and Sir William fighting a duel over Emma; and she could always say that people who would believe something so false and ridiculous would believe anything. The lovers would naturally be discreet and Emma was a superb actress. Knowing or unknowing – in either case not caring enough to make a fuss which would only worsen matters – Sir William became part of the triangular structure, *tria juncta in uno*; the three-in-one which was to stand for seven years.

Sir William had other worries. By aiding the English before the battle, and openly rejoicing in its result, Naples had invited retaliation from the French, and was now threatened by invasion from without and by revolution from within and chances of a successful resistance were slight. The majority of the nobility imagined that by cooperating with the French they might preserve some of their ancient privileges, and their property. There were a few among the poor who retained some loyalty to Ferdinand if not to Maria Carolina, but the Liberty, Equality and Fraternity which the French promised was tempting to the underprivileged, and revolution offered a free-for-all looting; even the small middle class with whom the Queen was personally popular could not be trusted; most revolutions everywhere were headed by people of

(opposite) Maria Carolina, Queen of the Two Sicilies, daughter of Maria Theresa of Austria, sister of Marie Antoinette of France and Emma's close friend. Her husband King Ferdinand IV left the reins of government in her hands.

The *tria iuncto in uno* ridiculed by Gillray. It is not hard to guess the allusions in the objects the 'Cognocenti' (Sir William) is contemplating. Cleopatra, topless and clutching a gin bottle, clearly alludes to Emma, Mark Anthony to Nelson, and Claudius bedecked with a cuckold's horns to Sir William himself.

the middle sort. It was true that the English government, aware of the danger to Naples, had ordered Nelson and his ships to stay in a protective capacity, but apart from a few marines he had no men with any experience in fighting on land. It was soon apparent that if the King and Queen of Naples were to escape the fate of Louis XVI and Marie Antoinette, they must seek safety elsewhere. Sicily seemed to be the obvious refuge since it was only open to attack from sea and the English ships were capable of dealing with anything seaborne which the French could muster at the moment, and the Sicilians were a peculiar people who could be counted upon to take a line different from that pursued in Naples. They were fierce, rough people, much interbred, among themselves they could carry on a vendetta from generation to generation, but they were intensely nationalistic. Ferdinand, at least was sure of a welcome there, it was his childhood home.

The move must be made with the greatest secrecy; the lesson of Louis and Marie Antoinette's abortive flight had not been lost. For the King and Queen to quit the capital at a moment of crisis would further lower the morale of the troops, just about to go into action, and encourage the rioting among the pro-French rabble, already out of control.

Nelson made the plans, Emma to a large extent was responsible for putting them into action. Nobody knew how long the Sicilian exile might last, or how it would end, so the Royal Family and Royalists who intended to go with them must take every bit of portable value that could be collected and shipped. Much of it passed through Emma's hands. There were secret passages between the Embassy and the Royal Palace, and one between the Embassy and the shore. Sir William collected the choicest of his life long collection and had his treasures put aboard the *Colossus*. He meant to give them to the British Museum, but the *Colossus* sank in a storm and articles worth £10,000 in money went to the bottom. The real loss was greater from the antiquarian point of view and Sir William's grief was measureless; he was at an age where people tend to attach an extra importance to possessions, and he had collected and cherished so many beautiful, rare things.

When all was ready, it was arranged that the nucleus of the Royal party, Nelson and Emma, should slip away under cover of a party. (Perhaps Napoleon remembered this ruse when, seventeen years later he escaped from Elba during a theatre show.) The Sultan of Turkey had decided to honour Nelson by giving him the Plume of Triumph and his emissary, Kelim Effendi had come to Naples to present it. Egypt was at the time a Turkish province and the Battle of the Nile had saved it from the French. The presentation was made, the reception was in full swing when certain important guests slipped away. It was just ten o'clock.

Emma led the Royal Family by twisting subterranean passages and stairways to the shore, where they were met by Nelson's men and taken by barge to *Vanguard*, his flagship; Emma joined Sir William, her mother, Fatima and other members of her household and they used their own barge. By midnight on the 21st of December, they were all safely aboard.

It was a scene of utter confusion. The Royal party was large; the King, the Queen, their eldest son, his wife and new born baby, two princes, three princesses, nurses and other attendants. Sir John Acton was there because the Neapolitan Navy was either in open revolt or merely waiting for the French to come and take over. Boxes and bales of treasure lay about everywhere. Maria Carolina had broken at last, convinced that in leaving Naples she had been guilty of dishonour. It was in this hurlyburly that Mrs Cadogan showed her worth and gained from the King, high praise; 'She is an angel', he said. She, at least, could tell a box of bed linen from a box of bullion, and set about making beds and organizing things.

Maria Carolina once said of her husband that he never felt anything but self-love. Proving the truth of that statement, he now in this crisis, drew Sir William aside and promised him good shooting in Sicily, it being just the season for woodcock.

Admiral Sir John Acton was still capable of being shocked; he saw the baby's wet nurse suckling it. 'A sucking child makes a most dreadful spectacle', he recorded. Such a revulsion, felt at such a time, goes far to explain why, until saner notions became fashionable no woman who could possibly afford a wet nurse, breast fed her own child.

Then to add to the general misery a storm sprang up, the worst, Nelson said, that he had experienced in thirty years at sea. *Vanguard* and the ships with her, were unable to make for Palermo, but lay about in the Bay, tossed like the cockleboats of which Nelson had once written. Most people were seasick. Emma, living on her nerves, strung to concert pitch, was not, and went about doing what she could to comfort and alleviate. The stench alone must have been formidable; a warship – its ordinary sanitary accommodation averaging one *seated* lavatory to a hundred men must have offered scenes more disgusting than a baby at the breast.

When the storm was at its worst, Emma missed her husband and went in search; she found him in a small cabin, a loaded pistol in each hand. He explained that he would sooner shoot himself than have salt water go guggle-guggle down his throat. He survived; the only recorded death during that terrible time, is that of the younger prince, six years old, and ailing when brought aboard. He went into that state which so often described the death-throes of the young, convulsions, and Emma, who was fond of him, held him in her arms as he died.

It is all over and done with, an old threadbare story, but something sparks still. Apart from everything else, every service Emma had ever done her, should not Maria Carolina have remained everlastingly grateful for that one act of kindness?

It was snowing when they finally reached Palermo; the weather seemed to have gone wrong. Like many places south of Rome,

Early in 1799 the royal family fled secretly from a pro-French mob across the sea to Palermo in Sicily. Emma's resourcefulness was largely responsible for the successful escape, and her bravery was reported in *The Times*.

Sicily was not equipped for a cold winter, no fireplaces, no chimneys. And Palermo itself was not equipped to deal with an influx of refugees – in all about two thousand arrived – there was one inn, but twenty-two religious houses, willing to offer space and hospitality – at a price. Sir William, having recovered from his suicidal fit and one of his usual attacks of bilious fever, pulled himself together and remembered that he was still the British Ambassador, responsible for the English who had fled Naples, and any English who might arrive. For French-born refugees he could do nothing. The Sicilians were so anti-French that they would not allow any of the French aristocrats who had taken refuge in Naples and were now forced to flee again, to land. Nelson was obliged to make arrangements for them to be taken to Trieste – Austrian territory at the time. In January a French ship, carrying wounded and sick from Egypt to France sought shelter from a storm in a Sicilian port; the Sicilians killed 87 of the 140 men on board, and, so the story went, ate their livers, roasted.

By contrast the English were popular, provided they could pay the inflated prices – 100 per cent increase was usual. Sadly, Sir William reckoned what his sojourn in Palermo was costing him; he was obliged to hire a place suitable for a temporary Embassy, he must entertain, as usual. Sadly he listed the treasure that had gone down in the *Colossus* during the storm; and sadly he wondered what was happening to his home in Naples. He felt the cold, he had another bilious attack; he decided that he was too old for his post, and he changed his mind about spending retirement in Naples; he wished to go home to England as soon as he could. Through this miserable time, he took comfort in Nelson's company, of which he had a good deal as he had invited his friend to regard the Embassy as his home when ashore. 'I love Ld Nelson more & more – his activity is wonderfull and he loves us sincerely.' Nelson had been made a baron as a reward for his victory and though there were formalities still to come, he had chosen his title; Lord Nelson of the Nile.

Sir William might well worry about the Palazzo Sessa. Naples was in the hands of the mob, then of the French who made some attempt to restore law and order, which the mobs resented, the looting and the carnage had been so enjoyable. Some Neapolitans formed small underground groups and were so dangerous that Frenchmen, supposedly in control, dared not walk the streets alone.

In later years those who ridiculed the service Emma had done the Queen should have consulted *The Times*. On 28th of January 1799 it reported the flight to Sicily, and nine days later said, 'We are informed from a very respectable authority that the Queen owed her safety much to the address of Lady Hamilton, who assisted in her getting away.'

Maria Carolina was safe, but wretched at what she regarded as the loss of her Kingdom; she had lost a child in the flight, and, final misery, Ferdinand chose this moment to lay the blame for the whole situation on her and her fondness for the English. None of this would have happened had Naples stayed strictly neutral!

Besides the uncontrollability of the Neapolitan mob, there was another factor which the French had disregarded – religion. The Neapolitans were deeply religious in their own way, which was riddled with superstition, and not much concerned with moral behaviour. The French were declared atheists; early in the Revolution they'd crowned a pretty prostitute on the altar of Notre Dame, calling her the Goddess of Reason. They had driven out the priests, broken with the Pope; they might well be regarded as the followers of anti-Christ.

There was one man in the countryside north of Naples who saw in religion a lever and a way to power. Cardinal Ruffo was a Prince of the Church and the owner of vast estates in Calabria. He sent out a call for recruits for the Christian Army, and soon had 17,000 men. Many of them were his own tenants and he knew just what to promise them, relief from taxes, unlimited looting, and a chance to fight against the Devil.

Other resistance was being organized, too: professional bandits disliked the prospect of French rule; they coalesced under the leadership of a ferocious man known as the Big Devil. Both these makeshift armies stood between the French in Naples and the

(left) The French had entered Naples in January 1799 and were welcomed by the liberals who set up the Parthenopean Republic.
(right) In June 1799 Cardinal Ruffo's Christian Army, with some help from bandits and guerillas, liberated Naples from the French. Ferdinand, safe in Sicily, sent Nelson to control Ruffo, whose treaty with the French he declared invalid.

French-held territories across the border. In June the English Fleet blockaded the port of Naples, and the end was inevitable. Cardinal Ruffo's Christian Army, with some help from bandits and guerillas, liberated Naples later in the month, and all the more horrific scenes of Paris during the Terror were repeated. Cannibalism is mentioned again. The French signed a treaty with Ruffo which was to lead to bitter dispute. French soldiers were to be given the honourable treatment due to prisoners of war. Neapolitans who had collaborated with the French were misled into the belief that a similar amnesty would be given to them. Instead they were treated as rebels and traitors. And to confound confusion, Ferdinand, safe in Sicily, declared that Cardinal Ruffo had no power to make a treaty at all, and sent Nelson to Naples to control the liberator, if necessary even to arrest him.

What took place that summer in strife-torn Naples was held against Nelson, to whom authority had been delegated, and against Emma, who, with Sir William, had gone along to act as interpreter. There were atrocities, and there were executions, but Nelson actually signed only one death warrant – that of a Neapolitan naval officer who had gone over to the French and who was tried and sentenced by a court-martial composed entirely of Neapolitan naval officers who had remained loyal to the King and Queen. 'Lady Hamilton has not been remiss in adding her quota to the barbarity that inflames every breast', wrote a lady who was nowhere near Naples at the time, and who relied for her misinformation upon a man with whom Nelson had already had a furious row about the provisions provided to his ships. A man deprived of his 'perks' can be a vicious enemy.

It is cruelly ironic that Nelson should have been called inhuman. He was the ideal commander, always leading 'by love and example'. There is proof that his men loved him in the fact that although there were ominous mutinies in other English ships and fleets, there was never a mutiny in any ship, or group of ships under his command. His men knew that he had their welfare at heart, would never demand of them anything he was

(*opposite*) Nelson by Abbott. In his hat he wears the Plume of Triumph sent to him by the Sultan of Turkey in gratitude for saving Egypt (then a Turkish province) from the French.

not willing to do himself. As for Emma, she had such a compassionate nature that she hated to see even an animal suffer – an attitude most unusual at the time; she had always avoided going with Sir William on his shooting and hunting trips with the King where birds and animals were driven in Continental fashion, given no sporting chance, and slaughtered in vast numbers.

The year 1798 had been a glorious year for Nelson; 1799 saw him as he termed it, 'on the rack'. He was sent contradictory orders and at least one which was impossible to obey. How could he send marines to Minorca, when they were already on the mainland, fighting the French and the hard core of Neapolitan rebels who had held out in strongholds such as the fortress of St Elmo? His health was poor, he was subject to severe headaches and recurrent bouts of dysentry. His private life was a muddle. He was passionately in love with Emma, yet could see no future for them together. He still wrote to Fanny and received letters from her. He warned both her and his father that when he came home, as he hoped soon to do, they would see an old man. If any scandal had reached her ears, she had decided to ignore it and treat the whole thing as a momentary aberration; and his letters encouraged her in this attitude, since he told her to take a house in London against his return, and gave no indication that they would not resume life together.

Did Emma give serious thought to the future? She was in love again, after so many years; and this time with a far more rewarding lover than cold carping Greville. If the wholehearted exhuberance of young love could never be quite regained, there were ample compensations, for now she was in love with a hero, and could worship not only the man, but his reputation. The *tria juncto in uno* was firmly and happily established, and she would not have been human had she regarded any future confrontation with Fanny without complacency. She had been for so long, the most beautiful woman of her generation, so many men had desired her. She had good reason to feel confident.

(*opposite*) Nelson's favourite portrait of Emma, wearing the Maltese Cross, was painted in Dresden in 1800 by J. Schmidt. Emma was awarded the Cross in recognition of her services in securing supplies for Malta during the French occupation of 1798. The painting hung in Nelson's cabin on the *Victory*.

Nelson Recreating with his Tars, by Rowlandson. Nelson enjoyed an excellent relationship with his men. There was never a mutiny in any ship under his command, which makes it particularly ironic that Nelson should have been accused of inhumane actions at Naples.

Naples was a city which had been looted by the rebel mobs, sacked by the French, looted again by its liberators. Horses, carriages, pictures, all household goods had disappeared, only a few pieces of heavy furniture remained in the desolate palaces and villas. When the King decided to return to his capital city and take into his unaccustomed hands the reins of government, he made his headquarters on Nelson's flag ship. Maria Carolina remained in Palermo, and it was there, in the country which had never wavered in its loyalty, that the defeat of the French and the revolutionaries was celebrated. Visitors crowded in, and although Palermo was unaccustomed to such large-scale festivities, it rose to the occasion. After dark every window was lighted; there were huge firework displays, concerts and entertainments of the most lavish kind.

Gifts, too were the order of the day. Maria Carolina gave Emma a number of presents, mainly diamond-studded trinkets, one of them inscribed, *Eterna Gratitudine*. Sir William received a ring, 'a thumping yellow diamond'.

Nelson was given a sword with a golden, be-diamonded hilt; it had once been owned by Louis XIV of France. And he was also given a dukedom which carried with it an estate on the lower slopes of Etna. Weathered lava makes good soil – one reason why people return again and again to such perilous places – and the estate of Bronte, in the hands of a mercenary landlord, was capable of yielding £3,000 a year. Nelson was unworldly; he seems to have visited Bronte at least once, for later he spoke of its chestnut groves; he saw the dire poverty in which those who tilled the soil lived, and ordered that all income should be ploughed back in the form of agricultural improvement and social amenities.

He felt he could afford it. His barony ensured him £2,000 a year, and the East India Company, well aware of the significance of the Battle of the Nile, had made him a gift of £10,000.

Despite Maria Carolina's gifts, which were purely personal, Nelson thought that Emma's services had not been adequately acknowledged, so he asked Tsar Paul of Russia who was Grand Master of the Knights of Malta to make her a Dame of that Order. It was a courtesy title only and the decoration which came with it was, in Maria Carolina's opinion, such a poor thing, that she had it reset, with diamonds. Altogether the Queen's gifts to Emma were reckoned to be worth £60,000.

Reports of the jubilations in Sicily naturally reached the outer world and brought some curiously guarded letters from Nelson's best friends – naval men who had served with him. They warned him about the effect late nights, over-heated rooms and great banquets might have on his health. Nelson was too sensitive a man not to read between the lines. It was the danger to his reputation through his illicit love affair that they were concerned with.

Emma was at heart a gambler in the sense that she was willing to take a risk, and enjoyed the mild excitement of a game of cards –

Faro and Hazard being the most fashionable at the time; but the stories which began to circulate – often exaggerated by those who loved Nelson and chose to see her as the dangerous, deadly Circe, seducing and degrading him – were obviously untrue. They said that she sat up, late at night, playing cards, with Nelson, exhausted and yawning in the chair beside her, and that she would reach over and take as much as £500 from him and use it as a stake. It was nonsense; Nelson had not – was never to have – that amount

of ready money available. Nor was Emma the woman to be indifferent to the well-being of the man she loved. A good deal of card-playing did go on, for Maria Carolina, always a gambler, now played often and long in an attempt to divert her mind from what she regarded as her failure in life. When things settled down in Naples and Ferdinand went back, she wanted to go with him but he forbade her. She told Emma bitterly that Nature had designed her to be a mother and that she had merely put on the role of Queen as one dons fancy dress.

Fancy dress balls were extremely popular just then: Emma went to one, diaphanously clad, as the 'Favourite of The Harem'. It may have been an act of defiance – let them talk! It may have been the act of a woman, approaching the mid-thirties, anxious to display the famous sylph-like figure before it thickened, irreversibly.

(opposite) Fancy dress balls were extremely popular in Palermo as the Neapolitan court jubilantly celebrated the defeat of the French in Naples. Emma went to one diaphanously clad as the 'Favourite of the Harem', which may well have provoked comment from the press similar to Gillray's warning *(right) Ladies' dress as it soon will be.*

It was thickening from another cause when at last, after long delays, she and Sir William, and Nelson set out for home by a roundabout way which neither of them would have chosen. Both the men closest to Emma were frustrated men, checked, one in mid-career, the other toward its end. Lord St Vincent had retired and his place had been taken by Lord Keith, a man whom Nelson disliked and who heartily disliked him, but who must naturally be obeyed, so Nelson had spent some months after the liberation of Naples on relatively unimportant tasks, at odds with Keith who enjoyed checking his brilliant, successful subordinate, and dreaming of retirement. But to where? And with whom?

Sir William's resignation had been accepted and his successor appointed, rather prematurely, in Sir William's opinion; there were small, abrasive disputes about who was, at the moment, British Ambassador.

In the early summer of 1800, Maria Carolina decided to pay a long visit to Austria, taking two of her children and an entourage of fifty. Nelson, Sir William and Emma were to go with her, making their way overland to England.

The decision to make this protracted, exhausting journey must surely have been Emma's. Nelson would have preferred to go home, as a sailor should, in his own ship, and Sir William would have found a sea voyage far less trying. One feels that Emma already had a plan in mind and was set to carry it through, with, if nothing else, enormous bravado. She was already several months pregnant.

Lord Keith, then himself in the Mediterranean, was glad to see Nelson and Emma leave. 'Lady Hamilton has ruled the Fleet long enough', he said. The men in Nelson's ship felt otherwise, and probably spoke for the crews of other ships. They wrote:

My Lord, it is with extreme grief that we find you are about to leave us. We have been along with you (though not in the same Ship) in every Engagement your Lordship has been in, both by Sea and Land, and most humbly beg of your Lordship to permit us to go to England as your Boat's crew, in any Ship or Vessel, or in any way that may seem most pleasing to your Lordship. My Lord pardon the rude style of Seamen who are but little acquainted with writing, and believe us to be, my Lord, Your most humble and obedient servants Barge's Crew of the *Foudroyant*.

Apart from the ordinary hazards of eighteenth-century travel by road – wheels broke, or wheels fell off – the journey was uneventful, though once its course almost crossed that of the French Army. The family in Vienna gave Maria Carolina a warm welcome, but it was Nelson whom everybody wanted to see. His presence at a theatre guaranteed a full house, so in an effort to be just he attended thirteen in all; and there were banquets, never less than seventy people, at which his health was drunk while trumpets blared and cannon roared. He was the one man in Europe who had inflicted a real hurt upon Napoleon, and the more the French conquered on land, the brighter glowed the Battle of the Nile.

The stay in Vienna was prolonged because Sir William wilted and took to his bed for four weeks with one of his bilious fevers; but he recovered, and had the pleasure of fishing – his favourite outdoor pastime – in the grey waters of the Danube. Then the party moved on; to Prague; to Dresden. In Dresden there was a little shadow of things to come; the Electress of Saxony, a stickler for etiquette, refused to receive Lady Hamilton, though the Elector wished to honour Nelson. The British Ambassador to Saxony, embarrassed but tactful, explained to Emma that she would have found a visit to Court very dull, since it was to be a purely formal occasion, not a banquet. Emma is said to have cried, 'What, no guttling?' Not perhaps the most elegant of expressions, but now and then, when she was annoyed – and she would have seen through the flimsy excuse and been annoyed by it – she did employ a few pithy, countrified words, and *guttling* was little different from *guzzling*, which could be used with impunity.

CHAPTER
4

Home to England

Lady Hamilton did not dine at the Duke of Norfolk's last Sunday as mentioned in this paper of Monday; we are concerned to find her ladyship was indisposed.

Morning Herald
7 February 1801

The hero eventually arrived at Yarmouth on the 6th of November 1800, and was given a hero's welcome. Flags flew, bells rang and men took the place of horses between the carriage shafts. The party lodged at a modest inn, The Wrestlers' Arms, soon to change its name to The Nelson. There was the presentation of the Freedom of the Town, and a thanksgiving service in the church. In the midst of it all, Nelson found time to write two letters; one to the Admiralty, saying that his health was now fully restored and that he hoped his overland journey from the Mediterranean would not be construed as a wish to retire from active service. The other was addressed to Lady Nelson, Roundwood, Ipswich, Suffolk, saying that he and the Hamiltons would arrive there in time for dinner on Saturday.

Roundwood was a house which he hired, without seeing it, as a quiet country retreat for Fanny while he was away in the Mediterranean. She had tried living there, disliked the house and felt lonely, so she had given it up; she preferred London or Bath.

Except for working people who stuck to a mid-day dinner, the

(previous page) Nelson was given a hero's welcome when he arrived with the Hamiltons at Yarmouth on the 6th of November 1800. Flags flew, bells rang and men took the place of horses between the carriage shafts.

meal was a movable feast, three o'clock, four o'clock, gradually growing later, but Nelson and Emma and Sir William arrived at Roundwood while it was still light, even on a cloud-laden, storm-threatening afternoon in early autumn. Nelson did not know his way to Roundwood and the coachman was obliged to ask direction. When they arrived the place was shuttered and silent. Nelson's wife and his father were waiting to welcome him in London.

There was time to turn about and go to Colchester, where Mrs Cadogan and Fatima and the rest of their household already were. But what an end to a journey which had begun with an escort of mounted yeomanry. What a welcome! To a woman set about breaking up a marriage – and Emma undoubtedly was – what an opportunity to denigrate Fanny.

Next day they were in London, where Nelson met his wife and his father in the impersonal surroundings of a hotel. Then the Reverend Edmund, overwhelmed by emotion, pride and joy in his son, consternation at the situation, which probably only achieved reality at that moment; it is one thing to hear gossip, another to see its truth in the flesh, retired and the two married couples dined together at five o'clock. One can imagine how, both beautifully behaved, the two women eyed each other, like men bent on a duel. What did they see?

Fanny Nisbet, now Lady Nelson, was a woman of breeding, quietly elegant, totally self-controlled. She was well-connected

On their arrival, Emma was wearing a white muslin dress with 'Nelson' and 'Bronte' embroidered round the hem in gold thread and sequins.

Lady Nelson painted by
David Orme in 1798.
In complete contrast to Emma,
Fanny was a woman of breeding,
quietly elegant, and totally
self controlled.

and her first marriage, to a doctor, had been something of a *mésalliance*; but he had gone mad and died within a few months. After a more-than-decent interval she had married Nelson, always up-and-coming, and now arrived. She – perfectly acceptable everywhere – was the perfect wife for him. Opposed to her was the flamboyant, exotic woman who had climbed the social ladder by exploiting her sex. A woman now fat. Friendly observers had referred to Emma as a full-blown rose; others had called her a mountain of flesh, gross, enormous, but the most critical had admitted that her face was still pretty. Fanny could not know, few people were ever to know, that a good deal of Emma's bulk was due to her condition; plump women are never so obviously pregnant as thin ones.

It must have been a quite exceptional dinner party; the two women realizing that it was war to the knife, Nelson torn apart between the wife of whom he had once said that she had every quality desirable, and the mistress with whom he was infatuated; and Sir William, glad to have arrived in London at last, wishing it were bedtime. Fanny probably felt that she was in the stronger position; she knew Nelson's religious nature and high standard of honour. Back in England, subject to the influence of his very respectable family, might he not take the obvious, easy way and return, emotionally as well as physically, to his wife who had done nothing to offend him.

It was a vain hope. The nation's hero was as bewitched as a schoolboy with his first sweetheart. Indeed somebody said of him that in many ways he was a marvellous man, in others a baby. And he knew that Emma was carrying his child. It had been a grief to him to be childless and he was greatly excited by the prospect of becoming a father.

What went on between Fanny and her husband in private, what arguments, reproaches, cajoleries and explanations, we cannot know. For a little time Fanny seems to have copied Sir William's behaviour – see nothing; know nothing. Nelson went to the opera and sat in a box with Fanny on his left hand, Emma on his right, and with Sir William, the Reverend Edmund and Captain Hardy behind. The rise of the curtain was delayed while the audience applauded the hero of the Nile, 'Louder and longer than anyone could remember', Nelson had to bow and bow and bow. The orchestra played 'Rule Britannia', which had been Emma's theme song ever since the victory; she stood and sang with the others; Nelson's father broke down and cried.

Lady Nelson, a morning paper reported, was dressed in white, with a violet headdress decorated with a small white feather. Lady Hamilton wore blue satin and a plume of feathers. She was, the paper added, rather *embonpoint.*

It was a time of strain for them all. Nelson and Sir William went to Court and the King was ungracious to both of them. He asked Nelson if his health had recovered, was answered and then turned away to talk to some nonentity for half an hour. A distinct rebuff! And there was one for Emma in the offing. Lord and Lady Nelson and Sir William Hamilton were invited to Queen Charlotte's weekly Drawing Room. Emma was not included. Nor was she asked to dine at the table of those who were both fashionable and conventional. Lord and Lady Nelson were, of course, eagerly sought after and it was at an aristocratic table that Nelson showed his first sign of coldness toward his wife.

He was a man with one arm. Somebody had devised an implement which combined both knife and fork, and an admirer had sent him one, made of gold. With it he could manage most foods

Nelson's gold combined knife and fork was given to him by an admirer after he lost his arm at the Battle of the Nile.

though sometimes Emma and a few other very intimate friends were allowed to cut his meat for him. He could not peel a walnut. So Fanny peeled some, put them in a glass and had it passed to him. He pushed the offering away so violently that the glass broke, and when, a little later, the ladies retired, Fanny's rigid self control broke and she cried.

Nelson was very busy; he had to make his first appearance in the House of Lords; there were banquets given in his honour. He was helping Sir William to make a list of his losses at Naples and his expenses at Palermo – a total of £20,000. Sir William was, as always short of ready money, but he had not come back empty handed; *all* his treasures had not gone down in the *Colossus*. He was not prepared to sell anything immediately – dealers would take advantage of somebody anxious to sell. He wanted a gentleman's town house, where his lovely things could be suitably housed and displayed, discreetly inviting discreet offers. He found it. The ease with which accommodation, both furnished and unfurnished could be found in the eighteenth century is a source of amazement to the twentieth. For £1,000 down Sir William could take a long lease of 23 Piccadilly. It was unfurnished and to provide it with everything would cost, by Nelson's reckoning – and he was a rather frugal man – £2,500. So Emma sold her diamonds.

Reckoned in Sicily to be worth £60,000, they fetched £4,000 in London. Not that Maria Carolina's gifts had been unworthy of

(opposite) On their return to England, the Hamiltons leased 23 Piccadilly, one of the smaller houses facing Green Park.

(right) Nelson, Emma and Sir William spent the Christmas of 1800 with one of Sir William's relatives at Fonthill in Wiltshire, leaving Fanny alone in London with Nelson's father.

either the giver or the recipient; it was simply that the market was sluggish, possibly so many French émigrés had brought jewels with them and been forced to sell them in order to live. And of course Emma's eagerness to sell worked against her. Everything was done correctly; the lease was taken in Sir William's name; the furniture was Emma's. She was even more anxious than Sir William to have a place of her own; in January, at latest, she expected to be confined.

Then it was Christmas. Sir William's family on the whole had stayed loyal to him and William Beckford invited him, Emma and Nelson to keep Christmas at Fonthill. Fanny was left to spend a lonely Christmas, in a hired London house, with Nelson's father. She knew then that her marriage had failed absolutely; and next time she met her husband she gave an ultimatum; he must choose between Emma and her. If she had been only half as ill-natured as some accounts make her out to be, she would have offered the same hard choice to Nelson's father, but she did not.

In January 1801, Nelson was at sea again. The King might snub him, but the Admiralty knew his worth, and the threat of invasion from France had increased rather than dwindled. Nelson was given command of the Channel Fleet – another hovering, watchful, possibly inactive job. He was not worried about his own health, again bad, or about Fanny, or London society; he was intensely worried about Emma's approaching confinement, which he believed to be her first. All confinements were dangerous,

Ah where & ah where is my gallant Sailor gone', He's gone to Fight the Frenchmen for George upon y Throne. DIDO in Despair (He's gone to fight the Frenchmen t loose t'other Arm & Eye. And left me here with old Antique to lay me down & Cry.

A Gillray cartoon representing Emma after Nelson had gone to sea in January 1801. She was nine months pregnant, but society assumed that she was merely overweight.

and a first parturition at the age of thirty-five could well be fatal.

They had devised a method of communication which would leak nothing to naval censors or prying postal officials. In Nelson's ship there was a mythical sailor named Thomson – or Thompson – who had left his sweetheart, unmarried and expecting a child. Lady Hamilton had promised to keep an eye on the poor woman and send, through Nelson, news. When the child was born, she would be its godmother.

Writing as scribe for the illiterate Thomson, Nelson could say how worried he was, and how determined to marry his sweetheart as soon as he could. This was sheer fantasy. There was every

(opposite) On their return to England, the Hamiltons and Nelson often went to Drury Lane Theatre, where Emma's friend Jane Powell was a celebrated actress. In 1809 it burnt down and was later rebuilt to a different design.

likelihood of Sir William dying and leaving Emma a widow, but Fanny was only four years older than Emma and could not be expected to die just to oblige. In fact she outlived Nelson by twenty-six years, Emma by ten.

Toward the end of January, at 23 Piccadilly, Emma took to bed with a bad cold. Even in Naples she had suffered a cold now and then, and the English winter bore hard on those accustomed to a milder climate. Her mother was there, sensible and reliable as ever; there was Fatima to fetch and carry. How ignorant, indifferent or wilfully blind Sir William was it is impossible to tell, but there is one slender clue. Later on, whenever the child was brought to visit Emma, such visits were always carefully timed so as to coincide with Sir William's absence.

Unwanted children were all too easily disposed of at the beginning of the nineteenth century; many were simply put out to die of exposure; others died, a little more slowly, in the houses of baby-farmers; some were well cared for in homes not their own. Who recommended Mrs Gibson of Little Titchfield Street to Emma? It was a most fortunate choice, for she was not only conscientious but extremely discreet.

On an evening during the first week in February, Mrs Gibosn answered her door to a well-dressed lady who, once inside the house, produced from her muff a tiny baby and asked Mrs Gibson to take charge of it, promising that she would be well paid. The lady made no secret of her identity, she was Lady Hamilton, of 23 Piccadilly, and she was taking a kindly interest in the poor little orphan who had been born in the previous October. Mrs Gibson's experienced eye said otherwise; at most the infant was a week old. And that fact eliminated any possibility that the child could be Lady Hamilton's own. Childbirth was taken seriously by those who could afford to be self-indulgent; a month in bed was the rule; no woman of Lady Hamilton's standing would be up and out on a raw February evening within a week.

The child was to be known as Miss Horatia; no other name was given just then. Mrs Gibson accepted the charge and asked no

(opposite) Christie's Auction Room, by Rowlandson and Pugin. Sir William sold most of his collection of paintings at Christie's in 1801 in order to relieve his financial difficulties. The day's total was over £5,000.

questions; but she was puzzled; about the child's age, and by the fact that Lady Hamilton, who most certainly possessed her own carriage, should have a hired cab waiting in the street. Still, her business was to set about finding a wet nurse.

Emma went home, to continue coddling her cold and to write to Nelson. So far her plan had worked perfectly; that long journey across Europe had served its purpose in case any suspicion ever arose. How could a child, born in October, when Lady Hamilton was travelling from place to place and being, with Nelson, fêted everywhere, possibly be hers?

Nelson had word that Thomson's child was safely born and went almost mad with joy. He wrote that poor Thomson thought he would go mad with joy but dare not show his feelings. '. . . he has only me to consult with. He swears he will drink your health this day in a bumper and damn me if I don't join him in spite of all the doctors in Europe.' The last phrase referred to the advice given him by a doctor whom he had consulted about the failing sight in his good eye. He was to eat only the simplest of foods, avoid wine and even porter, do as little writing as possible, sit in a darkened room and wear an eyeshade. He had always been conspicuously moderate in his consumption of food and liquor, so the Spartan diet was no hardship; the other advice was impossible to follow while on active service, and now, with threatening partial blindness added to his other infirmities he began to think seriously of retirement. He and Emma would go to Bronte. 'This England is a shocking place', he wrote. There might be bandits in Italy, but it was better to be shot by a bandit than to have one's reputation stabbed. He took the way in which his King had treated him, and the way in which Society was treating Emma, very hard indeed.

Naturally when he visualized living in Bronte he included Horatia in his plans. He had the strongest possible paternal streak. It showed in his attitude toward his men; he visited them when they were sick and wounded. When possible he visited the relatives of those who died and once when a bereaved mother told him that her son had never received the medal due to him, he took off one of his own and gave it to her. That must have been a gift from the heart, for, feeling that on the whole he had been underrated he set a slightly disproportionate value on any tangible sign of esteem.

Horatia at about three years old.
She was born at Emma's London
house in January 1801.

After the birth of Horatia there is a slight switch, not of affection, but of attention, from Emma to the child. He was as utterly devoted as ever to the woman who had given him 'this dear pledge of love', the first he had ever had, the first, he believed, that she had ever given; but he was now father as well as lover; concerned about the quality of the wet nurse and – member of a clerical family! – about baptism; advising vaccination, in which he believed.

Since he, unlike Greville, did not preserve her letters, what she wrote to him can only be deduced from his replies. It is just possible that Emma knew that in the child she had a potential rival and wrote Nelson something of the kind of letter she had once written to Greville, letters to fan interest, to inspire a little jealousy. She certainly mentioned the Prince of Wales and Nelson reacted vigorously.

The Prince was now thirty-eight years old and if some of the beauty which had made people call him Prince Florizel, had vanished, he was still far from being the fat old man of the caricatures; and even when he did become old and fat, painted his face and wore corsets, he retained a singular charm. The marriage forced upon him had been a failure and his reputation where women were concerned was bad. Sir William, however, had good reason for cultivating the friendship of a Prince known to be, on any possible question, directly opposed to his father. So far nothing had been done about Sir William's pension – he had been promised £2,000 a year, or about his compensation. The Prince, himself powerless, had powerful friends and might get things moving. He was only too happy to receive overtures of friendship.

Gillray's cartoon of the Prince of Wales and Mrs Billington. The Prince of Wales was well known for his amatory exploits, and his attentions to Emma made Nelson frantically jealous.

Nelson wrote Emma some letters which he admitted were traitorous enough to get him hanged. He called the Heir Apparent, 'that villain', and 'that beast', and said, 'God strike him blind!' Writing as Thomson and referring to Sir William as Thomson's sweetheart's Uncle, he accused him of putting her up for auction. He begged Emma not to receive the Prince, or, if she must, to see that he was one of a large party. Nelson sometimes seemed to be naive, but he evidently knew the first moves in the process of seduction. If Emma entertained the beast, he would sit beside her at the table and their feet would touch! At the beginning, under how many tables had foot touched foot and set up that mysterious chemistry of desire? And Nelson was prey to the thought, the bugbear of men in his position; how far could Emma be trusted? It cropped up inevitably – unfaithful to X with me, why not unfaithful to me with Y?

Emma solved the problem by taking to her bed with a sick headache which made her incapable of entertaining His Royal Highness and his roving eye, his adventurous foot. And it was on this occasion that her husband made his single really ungallant remark about her. All her ailments, he said, were the result of her foul stomach.

To be sought after by the Prince of Wales was flattering, but Emma was set on something more – the conquest of Nelson's family. The first, most vulnerable target was his brother William who was Rector of an obscure Norfolk parish, Hilborough. Of all the children born at Burnham Thorpe, he had most advantages; he'd had the best education; he was a graduate of Cambridge, and having qualified for the Church had been given a very good living; his stipend at Hilborough was £700 a year. But he had exaggerated ideas of his own worth and a craving for promotion. He had a wife, Sarah, and two children, Horace and Charlotte. They had all been on friendly terms with Fanny, but had hoped that she would use her influence on her fine London friends to secure the longed-for promotion, and since she had failed to do so they were already disaffected before Emma appeared, with her charm, her potential power. In almost no time Sarah Nelson was Emma's great friend, her 'Jewel', and in conversation, in letters, they were making derogatory remarks about Fanny, who for some inscrutable reason was nicknamed Tom-tit. Now and again Emma wrote to the Reverend William, too, with just that touch of archness, coarseness, near flirtatiousness calculated to make an obscure, ageing cleric feel no end of a dog. Horace was at Eton – his fees being paid by Nelson, and Charlotte was at school in London. To both Emma was genuinely kind, whenever either had leave from school a welcome in Piccadilly was assured, glorious food, outings, presents. Emma's conquest of that family was complete.

Nelson's brother, Maurice, older than William, played little part in Emma's story; started off by his Uncle Suckling, he was a modestly successful civil servant. His wife had become blind, and when he died at the fairly early age of forty-six, Nelson made himself responsible for her. He and Emma were alike in their readiness to shoulder family obligations.

Nelson's eldest sister, Susanna, had married a man named Thomas Bolton, and there was a slight feeling that she had not done very well for herself. Thomas's brother was Rector of Brancaster on the Norfolk coast, but he himself was engaged in trade in Norwich at the time of his marriage – and not very successfully. He then took a farm and that was not very successful either, although the French war made many farmers prosperous. Kindly people said that the farm was too large for him; less kindly ones said that he spent too much time and money at the card table. The farm, at a place called Cranwich, near Brandon, was near the border between Norfolk and Suffolk, on sandy, unprofitable soil, wind eroded – farmers in the region say that their land is in Suffolk or Norfolk according to which way the wind blows. Crops on such soil are necessarily light, and acreage must be large to provide a living at all. Apart from his propensity to gamble there seems nothing to be said in Thomas Bolton's disfavour. He borrowed when able, he'd borrowed money from Fanny and was presently to borrow from Emma. There were six children, the oldest a boy, named Tom. For him the parents entertained moderate ambitions; they wished him to have a good education and looked hopefully to Nelson to assist them. What was eventually to happen to Tom only a soothsayer could have predicted.

The Boltons, simple, rather rustic people, were naturally shocked by the rumours that reached them, the more so because they liked Fanny, but they wished to remain on good terms with Nelson, so were obliged to accept the situation, and once they had met Emma, so kind, so hospitable and charming, they succumbed.

The William Nelsons and the Boltons may have been not entirely disinterested in their attitudes; the Matchams certainly were; they did not need financial assistance, nor did they crave promotion. Nelson's sister Catherine – twelve years younger than Susanna and nine years younger than Nelson, had made a good marriage. Her husband, George Matcham had spent some time in India, and as so many men did, had returned with a comfortable fortune, which he handled well. He had many interests and probably made even his hobby a paying concern. He liked to buy a house, exercise his cultivated, inventive mind on improving it, and then sell it, moving on to do the same thing with another house. The Matchams were a large family; Catherine had her first child in 1789, her eleventh in 1811, and in an age of appalling infant mortality, lost only one. The eldest Matcham boy, called George, was sure of a good education without any help from his famous uncle.

Mrs Matcham, between bearing and nursing children and moving house, had little time for purely social life, but the Matchams were a more mobile family than the Boltons, they kept a carriage, and could afford to stay in London. They, too, had been fond of Fanny, but they, too, were won over. Soon Fanny's only real partisan in the family to which she belonged, was Nelson's father, old and frail now, and obliged to leave his parish to a curate. He liked to stay with Fanny; she was a good nurse; but he liked Emma too. He was grieved by what had happened, doubtless concerned with the well-being of Nelson's soul, probably hoped for a reconciliation; but until he died he managed to keep a foot in both camps.

In late February Nelson had three days' leave. He stayed in a hotel, and went to Little Titchfield Street to see his daughter for the first time. Like many fathers-for-the-first-time, he was enchanted. Apart from that visit his leave had been disappointing; the lovers had not even had an opportunity of dining alone together. If they had, 'What a desert we would have had', Nelson wrote. (His spelling, though better than Emma's, could be unorthodox.) The sly innuendo in that phrase struck a note unusual for Nelson; his letters were emotionally rather than sexually charged. One wonders what Emma's were like. Even as a young woman, writing to Greville, she spoke of love rather than of sensual satisfaction. 'We was lovers' was about as near as she ever came to the verbal titillation which constitutes pornography and is the resort of the impotent and the frustrated. When he was sure that a letter could pass direct from his hand to hers, Nelson addressed her as his beloved wife, and so he thought of her.

That February leave was the prelude to an action which was to bring Nelson enormous personal fame, professional renown but misery of spirit. The war was running downhill towards a nego-tiated, tenuous peace when Nelson went, under the command of Sir Hyde Parker to fight the Battle of Copenhagen, designed to break Napoleon's hold on the Baltic. The objective was the Russian Fleet, but to get to it the English must pass the narrow strait between Denmark and Sweden; and the Danes had not only a lively navy but formidable shore-based guns. Too much for Sir Hyde Parker, ageing and not very venturesome; he gave the signal to withdraw. Nelson 'clapped his glass to his sightless eye, and 'I'm damned if I see it', he said. That is poetical licence. Both his eyes were now weak, neither was sightless, he merely dis-regarded the signal, and won another victory, but one with a

In February 1801 Nelson won the Battle of Copenhagen. Though probably his most daring exploit, for political reasons it was never recognized as such, a fact that embittered Nelson to the end of his life.

sour taste. There were those in England who said that the battle should never have taken place; that war with Denmark had never been openly declared, that peace with Napoleon who had closed the Baltic to English ships, was being negotiated. It was not the first time, nor would it be the last, when a man of action was to be decried by those who sat on Government benches and in counting houses. The lack of recognition of this, perhaps his most daring exploit, embittered Nelson to the end of his life. During the course of it, he spent some hours in an open boat, in bitter weather, and suffered such severe congestion of the chest that those around him were afraid that he had become consumptive.

In England, Sir William had sorted his treasures and decided what to sell, what to retain. Mr Christie explained in his advertisement that what he was about to sell was the collection of Sir William Hamilton who had spent thirty-seven years in Naples. Among the thirty pictures was one of Emma, and Nelson could not bear the thought of it being sold. How could the owner of such a treasure bear to part with it? He commissioned somebody to buy it for him, and Mr Christie knocked it down for £300, which was Nelson's limit. A Leonardo however reached £1,300 and the day's total was over £5,000, which was more than Sir William had expected. And he still had his vases – one which he had believed gone down on the *Colossus*. A private buyer bought the whole collection, privately, for £4,000. The wolf no longer lay on the doormat of 23 Piccadilly: and in addition Sir William was informed that he would have a pension; not the £2,000 a year for which he had hoped, but £1,300. He could afford to entertain and the William Nelsons were delighted to sit at table with noblemen, even if one of them was the notorious Duke of Queensberry.

Nelson was back in England in June 1801, happy, he wrote, to be on the same island as his beloved Emma. He came ashore at Yarmouth and went straight to the hospital where the wounded from the Battle of Copenhagen lay. The ordinary people gave him the usual wholehearted welcome, but in official quarters his latest victory was ignored. The whole thing had been so misunderstood that even Sir Hyde Parker, annoyed by the aspersions cast upon him, and by people demanding to be told why there had been a battle at all, demanded to be granted a court-martial; his request was refused.

Nelson was honoured by the Government, raised from baron to viscount. He added two words to his new title; he was now Lord Nelson of the Nile and of Hilborough, his brother's obscure little country village. His requests as to how the patent should be granted was proof that he recognized how much things had changed in three years. When, in 1798, he had first been ennobled there was no obvious reason why, given time, he should not beget a legitimate heir. Now it was different; he had broken with his wife and intended never to live with her again. Sir William might die, but while Fanny lived, no child that Emma bore could be regarded as legitimate. There was divorce, very difficult and complicated and unfair. It would have been possible for Nelson to have divorced Fanny for a single act of adultery; she could not divorce him for deserting her and living with Emma. The likelihood of a male heir to succeed to the title was remote indeed, so the patent was drawn up conferring the viscounty first upon the Reverend Edmund Nelson, should he outlive his son, then to the Reverend William Nelson, to his son Horace, to Tom Bolton, to George Matcham. 'Further than that I care not, it is far enough.' Privately, Nelson did think a little further. Unless something untoward happened, Horace Nelson would inherit and 'should he prove worthy' he could marry Horatia and make her Viscountess Nelson.

CHAPTER

5

Merton Place

It is altogether the worst place
under its circumstances that I
ever saw pretending to suit a
gentleman's family.
Surveyor's report on Merton

It was during this, another all-too-short leave that Nelson began
to plan for the more immediate future. He wanted a house of his
own. Forty-three years old, a peer of the realm, preeminently the
most successful man in his profession, he had never possessed a
permanent home. His aspirations were modest, as befitted his
purse and his character; he wanted a little place in the country,
not too far from London. It would also serve as Emma's country
house, so the place and all concerning it were to be left to her, but
everything, down to the last teaspoon, was to be bought with
Nelson's money. Nothing at all was to come from 23 Piccadilly.
The restriction shows both a nicety and an absurdity; presumably
it was permissible to take another man's wife, but not his household goods.

When Nelson returned to the Channel Fleet he left Emma with
the formidable task of finding a country house within easy reach
of London, obtainable for a down payment of £3,000, with the
promise of more to come. She set about the business with her

(previous page) Merton Place by Hawke Locker. On Nelson's instructions, Emma
found him a home, Merton Place, about six miles out of London in unspoilt
Surrey countryside. The house had no land of its own and little else to recom-
mend it as a suitable residence for England's hero.

usual energy, inspected various houses and settled on Merton Place in Surrey, about six miles out of London, but in unspoilt, rural countryside.

She was careful enough to ask a surveyor to look the place over and he gave it a most damning report. He described it as a poor low house, in bad repair, with only an acre and a half of its own, with other people's agricultural land pressing on both sides. On the ground floor there was only one room of any size, and above only one bedroom fit for a gentleman – and even that had no dressing room. Merton Place had no stabling, no kitchen garden, no wall against which fruit could be grown. 'In short', the surveyor concluded, 'it is altogether the worst place under all its circumstances that I ever saw pretending to suit a Gentleman's family.'

Bone's miniature of Emma was
painted for Nelson at about the time
she acquired Merton.

In Emma's hands, it became Paradise Merton. She chose it because Nelson wrote that he liked the sound of it. The surveyor had seen all its defects, Emma saw its possibilities. Nelson probably liked the sound of it because it was a poor low house; he always called it his farm. As opportunity occurred he bought the adjoining fields, so that presently Merton stood in thirty acres and had everything necessary to fit it for a gentleman's family, including water closets, a luxury at the time.

Emma spent lavishly on repairs, on reconstruction, and on

109

additions. The old interior she lightened by substituting plate glass doors for the wooden ones, she used mirror glass strategically. She had taste, formed by her years in Naples, and rather flamboyant to some English eyes, but she made Merton into a place which became in a very real sense a home. Nelsons and Matchams and Boltons all spent happy holidays there.

She made a garden, famous for its roses. Even Sir William's hobby was catered for; the river Wandle ran near and one of its little tributaries, choked and foul in the past, bisected the Merton garden. Cleared out and spanned by a picturesque rustic bridge it was a scenic asset and a place where Sir William could fish. It was a source of anxiety to Nelson who wrote that the water must be fenced in for safety's sake. He was visualizing his child in his home. But Horatia remained with Mrs Gibson and was brought to Merton for one day, during Nelson's Christmas leave. Not on the obvious day, Christmas, but on a day when Sir William was absent. Whatever may have been thought later about how much he knew or did not know, it is plain that those closest to him believed that he was ignorant of Horatia's existence – and intended him to remain so.

Merton was already commuter ground and several large houses in the neighbourhood were occupied by men with businesses in the city. They were delighted to welcome Nelson into their little community. Later there are indications that they liked Emma, too. She entertained lavishly – so lavishly that both Nelson and Sir William were alarmed by the cost. At Merton Emma mixed

her guests with a fine disregard of discrimination; artists and musicians, people from the theatre – not yet regarded as wholly respectable, old friends and some hangers-on from the days in Naples. But eminent men were to be found there too. Lord Minto, once Viceroy of Corsica, and an old friend and admirer of Nelson, spent a weekend at Merton and thought it utterly deplorable. He thought that such a collection and display of Nelsoniania in the man's own house was in the worst possible taste – it would have been different had Lady Hamilton made such an exhibition in her own house. Lord Minto could not know that Merton was Emma's house.

It was during this visit that Nelson, so modest where he himself was concerned, asked Lord Minto to use influence in order to promote his brother William's appointment to a deanery or a presbytery. Emma was delighted to write to Mrs William and tell her that Lord Minto had said that a bishopric would be more suitable; and that Lord Minto had admired Charlotte, who was staying at Merton at the time. Lord Minto did not admire Emma; he wrote to his wife that the way in which she made love to Nelson, openly, was completely disgusting.

Glances, words, even the intonation of voice which disgusted a weekend visitor, could they have escaped the husband's notice?

Sir William's will was not made public until his death, but it was drawn up in May 1801, and it is revealing. As he had promised, he left everything to his nephew, Charles Greville, who was to give Emma £300 as a gift, and then allow her, from the estate £800 a year. Mrs Cadogan was to have £100 as a gift and an

112

allowance of £100 a year. It was an adequate allowance – though less than Nelson was paying to Fanny; but Sir William must have known that it would not support Emma in the style to which *he* had accustomed her. After all she was the girl who had once thought a guinea a week generous, and who, even after her marriage, had felt guilty about wearing a dress costing £25. Sir William had shaped her and now, in his will he was relegating her to relative poverty. Emma's £800 a year was only £100 more than the Reverend William's at Hilborough and the William Nelson's always regarded themselves as poor. They depended upon Nelson for Horace's school fees – even for a new pair of boots. It is impossible not to suspect in Sir William's will a subtle form of retaliation. The more so as he knew how extravagant Emma was becoming. Sir William, proud in his turn, had insisted that when he and Emma stayed under Nelson's roof, expenses should be shared; and £400 for wine, for six months, seemed to him to be excessive.

In 1802 the Peace of Amiens halted the war. A peace, as somebody said, 'everybody is glad of and nobody is proud of'. All sensible men knew that it was a fragile, tenuous peace, a mere drawing-of-breath between bouts. But it did allow Nelson to come home and at Paradise Merton, mend his shattered health. Never robust, invariably seasick at the beginning of a voyage, he had survived three major wounds, a spell in the West Indies where 20,000 English soldiers and sailors died every year, and an attack of that killer disease, consumption.

Physically he benefitted from Merton, the peace and quiet, the regular meals and Emma's loving care. Mentally he was uneasy. Everything that had been done to make Merton commodious and beautiful had been expensive; and he, the least mercenary of men, was obliged to think often about money. He wanted to provide for

(opposite above) Lord Minto, once Viceroy of Corsica and an old friend and admirer of Nelson,spent a weekend at Merton. He thought both Emma's behaviour and the display of Nelsoniana were in the worst possible taste.

(opposite below) Visitors to Merton were dazzled by the souvenirs Emma had collected. Even during Nelson's lifetime factories were producing quantities of goods to commemorate his victories. Shown here are a silver cup presented to Nelson by the Turkey Company after the Battle of the Nile, and part of a tea service commemorating the Battle of Copenhagen.

Horatia and for Emma. He once expressed a fear that when he was dead, Emma would be poor. And Emma, poor, was almost inconceivable. Her generosity, her extravagance, her charity simply brimmed over. Nelson, himself sympathetic with disabled or unemployed sailors, hoped that hordes of them would not track her down to Merton and ask for help.

He had other worries, too. The lawsuit with Lord St Vincent dragged on; the victory at Copenhagen had not been properly acknowledged; the last duty assigned him, just before the peace, had been the destruction of French barges, collected at Boulogne and along the French coast, ready for the invasion of England. Not a successful operation, and it had brought one of his favourite juniors, Parker, a wound which after the tortures of amputation – no anaesthetic but rum – to a painful death. Parker had died, not aboard ship, or in hospital, but in an inn at Deal, where Nelson had visited him as often as possible. After Parker's death his father had arrived and said that he could not meet the inn's charges or those of the surgeons. Nelson made himself responsible for those, too.

It had always been Nelson's wish that his father should make his permanent home at Merton and early in the Spring of 1802 he wrote to Bath where the Reverend Edmund was staying with the Matchams, and pressed him to come. The old man replied that as soon as Catherine's latest baby was born he would make the journey and hoped to smell a Merton rose in June. He was bound on a longer journey. He died in April.

The Matchams had warned Nelson that his father might not have long to live, but Nelson did not go to Bath. He pleaded – with some justification – his own poor health, but fear of meeting Fanny probably lay behind his excuse. He guessed, correctly, that the Matchams would have informed her and that she would go to the deathbed. Fanny did not, however, attend the funeral at Burnham Thorpe exactly a week later. Nor did Nelson. The day of the funeral was the 26th of April, Emma's birthday, and this year it was to be celebrated in unusual fashion. Fatima, 'from Egypt, a negress, about twenty years of age', was to be given a splendid baptism, and Nelson's health was not so bad that he could not attend the ceremony in Merton church where Fatima entered with one name and emerged with five – Fatima Emma

The Reverend Edmund, Nelson's father, died in April 1802. Nelson did not attend his funeral for fear of encountering his estranged wife Fanny, who had cared for her father-in-law during his last illness.

Charlotte Nelson Hamilton. Such behaviour, in a man of strong filial feelings, strikes a discordant note, but it accords with his still-infatuated state. Emma's birthday must not be spoiled; Emma's plans must not be upset.

With the Reverend Edmund's death, Fanny lost her last hold on the family. Emma wrote wonderful letters to the Nelsons, the Boltons and the Matchams. Exhibitionists – and she had become one – write the best letters of commiseration; and with the commiserations went invitations; it was the Nelsons, the Matchams and the Boltons who enjoyed the June roses at Merton that year. And Mrs Gibson brought Horatia, just for one day, which again coincided with Sir William's absence. Then Mrs Gibson and Horatia were sent for a seaside holiday in Ramsgate while Nelson, Sir William and Emma stayed at nearby Margate.

The arrangement suited Nelson – he could see his daughter, often by seeming chance; it suited Emma who loved bathing; it did not suit Sir William. He had just finished a tour of his Welsh estates, very tiring, he would have preferred a few days of quiet fishing. For the first time we can pinpoint his dissatisfaction.

Some things are easier to write than to say, face to face with a person likely to be offended and fly into a temper, likely to interrupt; so Sir William and Emma had cultivated the habit of

Margate, where Nelson, Sir William and Emma stayed during the summer of 1802. Horatia and Mrs Gibson had also been sent for a seaside holiday to nearby Ramsgate, which enabled Nelson to see his daughter often.

writing little notes to each other, even when they were under the same roof. Sir William mustered his arguments. He wrote:

> I am arrived at the age when some repose is really necessary & I promised myself a quiet home & altho' I was sensible & said so when I married, that I shou'd be superannuated when my wife wou'd be in her full beauty and vigour of youth. That time is arrived and we must make the best of it for the comfort of both parties. Unfortunately our tastes as to the manner of living are very different. I by no means wish to live in solitary retreat, but to have seldom less than 12 or 14 at table & those varying continually, is coming back to what was become so irksome to me in Italy during the latter years of my residence in that country. I have no connections out of my own family. I have no complaint to make, but I feel that the whole attention of my wife is given to Ld N and his interest at Merton. I well know the purity of Ld N's friendship for Emma and me and I know how very uncomfortable it wou'd make his Lp, our best friend if a separation shou'd take place . . .

He went on to add, and perhaps the Reverend Edmund's death had made him conscious of mortality, that he had only a little longer to live and must be allowed to be his own master and to follow his inclinations. There must be no more of the 'silly altercations' which had troubled them lately. 'There is no time for nonsense or trifling. I know and admire your talents & many excellent qualities but I am not blind to your defects & confess to

116

having many myself, therefore let us bear and forbear for God's sake.'

A separation would not only be uncomfortable for Nelson, it would expose Sir William to further ridicule and remarks such as; I told you so. Or; what did you expect? It would not have suited Emma, either, for it would explode the myth of the *tria juncta in uno* and further damage her reputation. Men seldom separated from their wives – after ten years of marriage – because they were extravagant and entertained too freely.

It is significant that Sir William, even when writing frankly and privately, made no mention of infidelity; he complained that he was paid too little attention. It is likely that this complaint decided Emma to install Charlotte Nelson as a permanent member of the household. Charlotte at fifteen was old enough to leave school, not yet sophisticated enough to be fully at ease in worldly company. She and Sir William could pair off. And if, as was desirable – she was to acquire the polish which a knowledge of other languages could supply, what better practice could she have than conversation with an old diplomat.

Charlotte's parents were delighted by the arrangement. Under the wing of Lady Hamilton, their daughter would pick up airs and graces and stand a good chance of finding a husband.

In his letter Sir William was not explicit about the silly altercations. He did say that they had arisen recently, so he was more likely to have been thinking about Emma's extravagance than about a love affair three years old.

Already the peace with France was fraying, and in March 1802 just a year after the Treaty of Amiens was signed, the Lords were discussing defensive measures. Characteristically, Nelson did not talk; he sent a note to the Prime Minister – 'Whenever it is necessary, I am your Admiral.' Emma and all the family braced themselves for another parting.

Is it cynical to think that the love between Nelson and Emma continued at such white-hot heat because it was not subjected to the rub of day-to-day living? They had no time to grow bored with each other. There were long absences, during which faults were forgotten, virtues magnified, and each reunion was another honeymoon. Nelson must have known that Emma had faults, a slaphappy attitude toward money, a taste for raffish company, a

117

Emma with Charlotte Nelson, aged fifteen.
Emma installed Charlotte as a permanent member of the household
in the hope that Sir William, who was feeling neglected,
might find her a congenial companion.

coolness toward Horatia and sometimes a disregard for his own expressed wishes. Horatia caught smallpox, so the vaccination had been neglected, or ill-done. Such things would have irked him more, had he spent more time with her. As it was, there he was so often, back in his cabin alone with his favourite picture of her. Not a Romney but a portrait made by Schmidt, in Dresden, in 1800. In it nothing serves to enhance beauty; a kind of scarf covers her to the chin and her only ornament is the Cross of Malta; her expression is grave – no smile, no touch of coquetry, her eyes look out, wistful and sad. This was his Emma, in paint on his cabin wall, alive in his imagination and memory. What were a few trivial faults?

Sir William had been justified in grudging those lost fishing days in the summer of 1802. Toward the end of that year and during early 1803, he was frequently in poor health. In his day seventy-three was a more advanced age than it is now, and the English winter was trying to one who had spent so long in Naples. Also he had lost his zest for life. He may also have suffered a slight shock upon discovering, through an accident, possibly contrived by her – the state of Emma's finances. Her personal debts – nothing to do with Merton or housekeeping – amounted to £700 and her balance at the bank was twelve shillings and elevenpence. To this discovery he reacted in the proper way; he added to his will a direction that his executors were to pay her debts, leaving his gift to her and her annuity unencumbered. He also took the opportunity of giving the *tria juncta in uno* a final injection of credibility. He left to Nelson a portrait of Emma – a copy of Vigée le Brun's portrait, done in enamel. '. . . . a very small token of the great regard I have for his Lordship, the most virtuous, loyal and truly brave character I have ever met with. God bless him and shame fall on all those who do not say "Amen".' Even for a free-thinker like Sir William, the anteroom to death is a place of solemnity and it is unlikely that those words were written tongue in cheek.

As a gentlemen should, Sir William went back to his own house to die, and Emma and Nelson were with him to the end, one on each side of the bed. As soon as he died, Nelson, as was proper, moved to a nearby hotel, and Mrs William Nelson was sent for to keep Emma company and to console her.

CHAPTER

6

Death of Sir William

Our dear Sir William died at
10 minutes past Ten this morning in Lady Hamilton's and
my arms without a sigh.

Nelson to Davison

It is generally believed that excessive mourning originated with
Queen Victoria; in fact all the trappings were in vogue before she
was born. Emma, without waiting to know whether she could
afford it, bought black for herself and her whole household at a
cost of £185; she also bought special jewellery, worth £170. With
mourning clothes only sad ornaments of jet, or black enamel
could be worn, no gem stones. Mourners stayed in seclusion; even
little Horatia must be kept indoors at Mrs Gibson's until after the
funeral, which was to take place in Pembrokeshire, since Sir
William had expressed a wish to lie beside his first wife. Emma
did not attend, nor did Nelson, but he wore black and cancelled
all but official engagements.

Those who disliked Emma, and the artist Vigée Le Brun was
one of them, thought Emma's grief shallow and pretentious; but
when she said that she had lost a friend and a father, she was
using words with precision. And if she cast off the black veiling
and the crepe a trifle too soon, she had good reason. There were
many claims on her attention.

(previous page) 'A very small token of the great regard I have for his Lordship.'
The miniature of Emma by Bone after Vigée Le Brun, left by Sir William to
Nelson in his will.

The house in Piccadilly was part of Sir William's estate, and Greville, behaving despicably again, gave her notice to quit within a month. She found a house nearby in Clarges Street, and moved the furniture – bought with her money – into it, and began to make plans for a family party. All under the shadow of imminent war. Kitty Bolton was to marry her first cousin, Captain William Bolton, son of the Rector of Brancaster on the 18th of May. On the 19th Nelson was to be – surely belatedly – formally invested as a Knight of the Bath; Tom Bolton and Horace Nelson were to be his attendant squires. But England needed her Admiral and in the pre-dawn dusk of the 18th, the wedding day, he drove away again, headed for Portsmouth. A proxy had to be found for him at the investiture and nobody below the rank of knight could be considered. So William Bolton, who had come up to London to be married was given a hasty accolade and another branch of Nelson's family was pushed a step up the social ladder.

Nelson was embarking at Portsmouth and wishing to avoid the send-off from the crowd, went stealthily aboard his flagship, *Victory*, by way of the bathing machines, those caravan-like structures, which, pulled by a horse into belly-deep water, enabled ladies to get into the sea without exposing what amount of leg, arm and shoulder the bathing costume of the day revealed.

Between Sir William's death and the outbreak of war, Nelson had been able to do only one thing for his daughter and that was to have her baptized. He would have liked the ceremony to take place at Merton, but even now, with Sir William dead, it was better to have the baptism of a child, two-and-a-half-years old, and of no known parentage, performed elsewhere. Multiple baptisms, even multiple funerals often took place in the little church in which Emma and Sir William had been married. Eight children were baptized that afternoon, 13th of May 1803. Neither Nelson nor Emma was present, all was left to Mrs Gibson, who had instructions from Emma to give the Clergyman and the Clerk a double fee and to see that the entry in the register was taken out. Mrs Gibson misunderstood; she thought that Emma needed a copy, which was given, while the Register remained unmutilated, showing that Horatia Nelson Thompson, born on the 29th of October 1800 was baptized on 13th of May 1803. Her godparents were Lady Hamilton and Lord Nelson.

Nelson was on active service again and obliged to write carefully, referring to Emma as Mrs T. (Evidently Thomson had made an honest woman of her!) He wrote openly of his terrible home-sickness and sense of separation, other things must be more oblique. Emma was charged to tell Mrs T. 'that my love is un-bounded to her and her dear sweet child; and if she should have more it will extend to all of them . . .'

Emma was again pregnant. Perhaps Nelson could find some comfort in the thought that this was not a first parturition, but for Emma there was the long pretence that all was well, all the secrecy and stealthy management. Her growing bulk she at-tributed to drinking a great deal of porter, believed to be good for the voice. Prima donnas drank it between acts. Once even her courage failed, for she was now in a worse position than when Horatia was born; she now had no husband to lend his countenance should anything go wrong. Nelson was sailing toward the Mediterranean, and she wrote suggesting that she should join him there, bringing Horatia and Charlotte Nelson with her. Such a plan was impossible in time of war, and that she ever mentioned it showed a momentary loss of morale, but her spirit rebounded and she went off to stay with the Boltons at Cranwich, and then at Canterbury with the William Nelsons. The Reverend William had at last received the longed-for prebendary stall.

At Cranwich she must have noticed some financial stress, for afterwards she sent Susanna £100, and of course wrote to tell Nelson, to show how highly she regarded his family. He did not praise; he protested. How could she afford such a gift? 'It is

(right) Heavily pregnant again, Emma concealed her growing bulk with a shawl and continued to entertain. In this Baxter sketch she is singing a duet with Madame Bianchi, a musician she first met in Naples.

(centre) Sketch by Baxter of one of the Connor cousins who was living with Emma when Nelson's second child was born.

(far right) Charlotte Nelson, now of debutante age, was also staying in the house. Never a lay-abed, Emma quickly recovered from childbirth and the death of her baby to act as Charlotte's chaperone.

impossible out of your income.' In fact what Emma could afford
and what she spent no longer bore any real relationship. Nelson
at least did know when he was in debt and roughly to what
extent; and he worried about such things. Merton, which he had
visualized as a small country place, a farm, was already heavily
encumbered. He worried about Emma's future, and at the earliest
possible moment, wrote to the Queen of Naples – now reinstated,
if rather shakily – pointing out that her Majesty had never had a
more attached and real friend than Emma Hamilton, and that Sir
William had not left her 'in such comfortable circumstances as
his fortune would have allowed'. Maria Carolina had forgotten
her eternal gratitude and sent back a letter of a purely political
nature which infuriated Nelson. 'If she can forget Emma I hope
that God will forget her,' he wrote. He also wrote about Merton
and the expenses running up there; was this necessary? Was that?
And he wrote that he hoped that Horatia would be there for the
winter. (To twentieth-century people the migration of generations
of people who moved into London during the summer when the
countryside was at its best, and then back into the country
during winter, seems a bit odd, but there was sense behind it. In
winter, when everybody who could afford it had a fire of some sort,
and a house of substance might have a dozen, the smoke from a
conglomeration of chimneys mixed with the fog drifting up-river
to produce the aptly named pea-souper, was unpleasant for everybody and lethal to many young and to many old.)

Emma did not immediately bring Horatia into her household.
She did bring other young people, notably her Connor cousins.

Sir William had never liked them and possibly his judgement was sound. There were three girls, Sarah, Mary and Cecilia, and one boy who later went mad. The Connors were poor, but all the girls had been educated to the standard – not high, but for poor girls rather rare – where they could take posts as governesses. When Emma said that she had subsidized the Connor family to the extent of £2,000, she was probably speaking the truth, as she so often did, and was disbelieved. Sir William would not have a Connor in the house; now he was dead and the Connor girls flicked in and out, as housekeepers, or as governesses to Horatia when at long last she was brought home. Now Grandmother Kidd was dead that ill-fated, but well-educated girl, Little Emma, was regarded as one of the Connor family, but was not invited to London or Merton.

A Miss Connor was part of the household, so was Charlotte Nelson, when towards the end of the year, Emma took to her bed again, with, as she wrote to Mrs William Nelson, 'a soor throat cold and cough'. She was up and about again within eight days.

This time there was no need for Mrs Gibson's services and close-mouthed discretion. Nelson's second child was either born dead or expired immediately after birth, and was disposed of. It was so easy at the time. It was not long since Thomas Coram, a toughish sea captain had been so shocked by the sight of infants, dead, or alive, thrown on to rubbish heaps in the heart of London that he founded a refuge for unwanted children. Quite possibly another 'pledge of love', born of a liaison between the most beautiful woman, the most gallant man, of the age ended as a little crumpled heap of rubbish on a dump. One thing is certain, Emma would never have thrown it out alive. And the fact that this time she took so long to recover from her confinement indicates a stillbirth, always more troublesome than a live one. But she was never a lay-abed; she was soon up and doing and presenting very conventional hostesses with a problem. Charlotte Nelson was now of debutante age; she was the daughter of a clergyman, a prebend of Canterbury, a niece of the man upon whom all England's hopes were founded. She must be invited to this gathering and that, and a girl so young must be chaperoned. By whom? Obviously by Lady Hamilton whose protégé she was.

After the birth of Little Emma, Emma had regained her sylph-like figure, after Horatia was born she had become noticeably

It is amusing to compare Sherrard's caricature of Emma performing an Attitude *(left)* with an earlier drawing by Rehburg *(below)* to which the artist obviously alludes. After the birth of Nelson's second child, Emma never regained her figure, a fact that neither the empire fashions nor the cartoonists of the day did anything to disguise.

(below) In these drawings of Emma performing her Attitudes, she is noticeably *embonpoint* compared with earlier portrayals of her sylph-like figure.

thinner, this last birth left her with the beginning of the bulk which was to be so cruelly exaggerated by cartoonists, and the Empire fashions now in vogue were not kind to the stout, or those past their first youth. The rose was now slightly overblown, but she was not without admirers. There had always been more to her than prettiness of face and litheness of figure; she had charm – when she wished to employ it, a zest for life which expressed itself in a fondness for the pleasures of the table, in hospitality, *bonhomie*, a desire that everyone about her should be happy and comfortable.

To maintain her way of life more money was needed than was available, and at this time she began to bombard the government with what are called her 'Memorials'. They were not, as the name implies, anything to do with the dead; they were a summing up of services rendered to her country, expenses incurred in those services, and a request for compensation. Among other things she claimed that she had given £6,000 to buy corn for the starving people of Malta. Sceptics demanded to know where the wife of a not over-rich man could have obtained such a sum of money. Such people ignored the fact that Emma did not need to have money in order to spend it. When the Maltese were starving after a long siege, Emma was the close friend of the Queen of Naples, and the wife of the British Ambassador; her credit was good. Corn was certainly sent. For her other claim, coaxing Maria Carolina to support the British Fleet, Nelson himself was witness.

Nothing came of this first Memorial, nor of any subsequent one. Of the successive Prime Ministers to whom Emma appealed, only Pitt regarded her claims with sympathy, and he died before he could give evidence of his goodwill. The reason for the rejections probably lay with the King; George III may not even have spoken a word directly concerned with Emma, but his ministers knew his feelings about the *tria juncta in uno*. His behaviour to Nelson and Sir William had made it very plain, and George was a pig-headed man, unlikely to change his mind.

Later on the Memorials became less realistic and more hysterical; Emma was like a child, screaming for attention, and screaming more loudly when the attention was not forthcoming. She screamed on Sir William's behalf, too. He had never had the full pension for which he had asked, and he had never received a penny in compensation for what he had spent in Sicily while performing his duty in difficult circumstances.

The finances of the early nineteenth century are difficult to understand; even an expert admits the situation to be 'fairly unclear'. We know that the pound was worth about six times as much as it is today, but the long war was causing inflation. In a short time the cost of living had doubled, and indirect taxation was imposed 'on everything that moves'. Horses, carriages, gigs, menservants, all were taxed. Things that did not move were not exempt; hearths, if there were more than one in the house, windows, playing cards. Then there was that obnoxious thing, Income Tax, levied for the first time, and something almost as hateful to people accustomed to jingling coins – paper money.

At the same time it was fatally easy to get into debt. There was so much competition for customers that a title, a known name, a good address, even an assured manner and decent clothing, enabled people to run up bills, or to borrow money. To press for payment of a bill was to lose custom, accounts sometimes ran on for years and naturally the creditor was bound in self-defence to reimburse himself – a shilling here and there on a bill, a charge for some item never supplied. Emma, who when she had £20 had given £5 away was ill-equipped to deal with such a situation. She was too optimistic; her claims, Sir William's claims on the Government would be acknowledged; Nelson would win some Prize Money . . .

Nelson was thinking about money, too, but less optimistically. He was concerned about something Emma disregarded – the

Of the successive Prime Ministers to whom
Emma appealed, only Pitt regarded her claims with sympathy,
and he died before he could evidence his good will.

future. He was worried about Horatia; she had no producible parents, and only a decent dowry could compensate for that disadvantage; yet the most he could leave her was £4,000. He had received his gift of £10,000 from the East India Company; out of it he had returned to Fanny the £4,000 that had been her dowry and had paid the first instalment on Merton's price and provided basic furniture. The £2,000 which went with his title, and his pay were gobbled up by his allowance to Fanny, to the blind widow of his brother Maurice – and by many more unrecorded commitments. The most that Horatia could be certain of was £4,000 and that must be protected, placed on trust, safe from Emma. While the child remained in Emma's care, Emma could use the interest; the capital she could not touch. He wrote quite bluntly about it, 'I shall put it out of your power to spend dear Horatia's money'.

Mrs Cadogan was worried about money in her down-to-earth way. She had taken up her residence at Merton, she liked the country and enjoyed better health there than in London. She was a careful manager, but even she was obliged to write to Emma to say that the butcher's and baker's bills now totalled over £100 and that the gardener and his assistant had not been paid. Nelson was paying £100 a month towards Merton's upkeep, and he had so often expressed his horror of debt that Emma dared not tell him that she had overspent. Presently what she called her 'little debts', amounted to £530. A Mr Davison, a man of business, and a friend of Nelson's, who dealt with all his affairs, paid the bills for her, with admonishments to thrift in the future. She was now incapable of it, and was gambling more, not for fun, but like Thomas Bolton, in the hope of recuperating her fortune. One can only deduce that she too, was an unlucky gambler.

Nelson was also unfortunate. This, his second spell of duty in the Mediterranean with a watching brief, was an unremunerative business, but he did capture one rich prize and his share should have been substantial, but over a technicality, he was defrauded, as he had been over the Battle of Cape St Vincent.

At the beginning of the second stage of the war, Nelson had said that it would not be a long war, but it dragged on. Watchful as Nelson was, and eager for action, the French Fleet eluded him in thick fog and went off to the West Indies. Nelson followed, and although no major action took place, the English ships once again saved the valuable islands and prevented the French who outnumbered them two to one from landing. There was a period of no news; some reports said that Nelson was in the Eastern Mediterranean. Worry brought on Emma's nettle rash and she went with friends to Southend and bathed. She did not take Horatia with her; nor had she done as Nelson constantly urged, taken the child to live at Merton permanently. In fact where Horatia was concerned she seems to have suffered what is now called an emotional block. It even prevented her from paying Mrs Gibson regularly, though Nelson always earmarked money for this purpose. At one point £30 was owing – a large sum in the budget of a poor woman. It seems that Nelson suspected Mrs Gibson of being obstructive for he had written to his solicitor that he wished Mrs Gibson to have an annuity of £20 on condition that 'she gives up my adopted daughter Horatia Nelson Thompson to the Guardianship of My Dear Friend Lady Emma Hamilton and promises not to have anything more to do with the Child, either directly or indirectly and I leave my estate chargeable with this Annuity'.

It is just possible that he was right – he had more than once shown an almost uncanny insight into the minds of other people; and there could have been a reason – besides her lack of maternal feeling – for Emma's dilatoriness in bringing the little girl home. Mrs Gibson did not know much, but at least she knew that Horatia was not four months old when she was brought to Titchfield Street and Nelson, on his first visit there had not behaved like a man viewing another man's child. And quite apart from the money foster-parents do often become attached to children whom they have watched develop through perhaps the most entrancing stages; the first word, the first tottering step make ties not easily broken.

In Mrs Gibson's case the ties were broken, abruptly, in August 1805, for with dramatic suddenness, Nelson came home. On the 18th he wrote from Spithead.

> I hope we shall be out of quarantine tomorrow, when I shall fly to dear Merton. You must believe all I would say and fancy what I think, but I suppose this letter will be cut open, smoked and perhaps read . . . I have not heard from you since April . . . The boat is waiting and I must finish. This day two years and three months I left you. God give us as a happy meeting as our parting was sorrowful.

Nelson's Last Leave

At his table he was the last heard among the company, and so far from being the hero of his own tale, I never heard him voluntarily refer to any of the great actions of his Life.

George Matcham

Hindsight is an indulgence, but it is pleasant to think that this, his last leave, was so happy, bringing together all the people he loved in the place he loved. He and many other sailors had been called home because Napoleon was once again threatening to invade; they were given leave, just long enough to get their shore legs, see their families, settle their affairs. Nobody knew how long the leave would last; a week? ten days? Everybody knew that though he might be overlooked when Prize Money was being allocated, when it came to fighting, Nelson was the man, the first on call.

Emma snatched Horatia from Mrs Gibson, and sent out invitations to all the family. Reconstruction work was still going on at Merton and occasionally Horace Nelson and Tom Bolton, whose fates were to be so entwined, had to share a room. George Matcham was there too, a rather critical teenager, noting everything and sometimes disapproving.

It was Horatia's introduction to Nelsons, Boltons and Matchams, and they accepted her, not, as Nelson said, as his adopted child, but as his own. Portraits show the strong likeness

(previous page) Card parties at Merton by Baxter. Emma did not gamble merely within the family, and she was soon to amass large gambling debts.

134

Horace Nelson, Nelson's nephew and heir, is on the left of this group. Nelson hoped he would marry Horatia, but he died of typhoid fever in 1806.

between them, and his manner towards the child was altogether too doting. Nobody suspected the real relationship between Emma and her daughter; that secret had been well-kept, and although Nelson seeing the infant for the first time had said that she resembled her mother, either he had deluded himself, or the child had changed. Then there was the date of her birth, October 1800 when Lady Hamilton was on her way back to England, with quite an entourage; how could she have had a baby then? Also to be considered was Lady Hamilton's fondness for and willingness to take care of young people, not only those of Nelson's family, and her own, but complete strangers like little Mary Gibbs. That young orphan had been deliberately brought into Emma's care, on the principle that the best place to hide a leaf is in a forest.

Even in this moral family, the double standard was acceptable; the beloved brother, away from home for such long periods and in such strange places, had made a slip, and the result was this charming little girl, well taken care of and greatly loved. He had done all that he could to repair his fault. Everybody could be happy about it.

The fond father went to London, kept four important, high-level appointments, but found time to order a set of cutlery, engraved with Horatia's name, and a silver-gilt drinking cup, bearing the words; 'To my much-loved Horatia'. It is more than likely that he also ordered the rocking horse beside which Horatia was painted; a tall mount, its saddle level with her shoulders.

This, his last leave, showed Nelson as he would have been, had he lived and retired, a happy family man, a contented small country squire. He took interest in the poorer villagers and expressed a wish that nobody in Merton should suffer distress or privation within his power to relieve. He made his gifts anonymously, through the vicar, Mr Lancaster. He went to church regularly, taking Horatia with him. Mr Lancaster thought so highly of him that he asked him to take his twelve-year-old son into his ship as a First Class Volunteer, when he returned to sea.

Despite, or perhaps because of, Nelson's eminence, the Press could not let the old scandal die, but if the innuendoes and double meanings were ever brought to Mr Lancaster's attention, it was easy to discount them. Both Emma and Nelson took great pains to preserve a facade of respectability. Merton was Nelson's home; when he was at sea she stayed there, supervising the work of improvement, keeping it lived in; when he was at home she was a guest there – always with others. She had her own house in Clarges Street, and there Nelson was the guest, among others, and on apparently similar terms. He did not sleep there. At Merton there was Mrs Cadogan, the very image of respectability, the ideal custodian. And would the Reverend William Nelson, a prebend of Canterbury have entrusted his daughter, Charlotte, to the care of a woman of low reputation?

Horatia with her rocking horse, by Baxter.
(right) Horatia's drinking cup bearing the
words 'To my much loved Horatia',
ordered by Nelson for Horatia shortly
before the Battle of Trafalgar.

Lord Minto again visited Merton which he found much
improved – though the Nelsoniana had not been reduced. He was
the one who said that in some ways this great man was a baby,
meaning that this battle-scarred veteran, a hero, forty-seven
years old, was still in love, like a school boy.

Sir William had complained about the number of dinner guests;
during those mellow late summer, early autumn days of 1805
there were sometimes so many that a second table was needed and
the guests ranged from the Duke of Clarence – twenty-five years
later to be William IV, England's bluff old Sailor King, to an old
Kidd relative from Wales. He rather lowered the tone by going
down to the public house and getting drunk with the locals.
Typically, it was Mrs Cadogan who was mortified by such un-
seemly behaviour.

The Duke of Clarence, later
William IV, the Sailor King,
was one of the many and varied
guests to visit Merton in the
autumn of 1805.

In later years it was George Matcham, never quite dazzled by
Merton, and critical by nature, who gave a good description of
his famous uncle, 'quiet, sedate and unobtrusive'. A man in a
plain dark suit, kind and considerate to everybody, 'chiefly those
who seemed to require it most'. Nelson's voice was the last to be
heard at his own table; he never referred to his own exploits,
when he did talk he showed a caustic sense of humour.

In these days of the anti-hero, Nelson does sound almost too
good to be true; perhaps whatever power arranges these things
provided a surreptitious love affair as a healthily human counter-
balance. It was still surreptitious, and must be so while Fanny
lived, and that kept the fires alight. Most of the best love stories
have been secret. How often at Merton, with the house full of
guests, did they retire separately and wait, and listen until all
was quiet? How often did Nelson leave Clarges Street with his
fellow diners and then turn back? If the theory that strongly felt
emotion leaves an impression on places, something that can be
played back in the form of psychic phenomena, both Merton
and Clarges Street should be haunted, by footsteps, by the
whispered endearments that lovers use. There is no evidence of it.

Over those sunlit days, the gradually chilling nights, hung the
imminence of war, of further battles to be fought. Nelson had an

interview with Pitt, who was Prime Minister, to discuss tactics. Pitt asked who should command the operation, which it was hoped would end the invasion threat and break the French Navy. Nelson said, 'You cannot have a better man than Collingwood.' 'No,' Pitt said, 'that won't do. *You* must take command. When can you be ready?' Nelson said, 'I am ready now.'

In a way these words, spoken in September make nonsense of the tale that Emma told later, about his reluctance to go and how she had to persuade him; but the two accounts are not necessarily self-contradictory. Two or more men can exist side by side in one man's hide and there was the Nelson, unequalled as a seaman, anxious to go; there was the Nelson so happy at Merton with Horatia and Emma; perhaps even a third Nelson who knew that no man's luck could last forever and that as a combatant he had already had rather more than his share; perhaps even a fourth, the son of the parsonage who knew that he had sinned and the wages of sin were death.

The call came and he left Merton at half-past ten on the evening of the 13th of September. He intended to travel through the night. Horatia was asleep and could have no knowledge of the parting, how her father kissed her and knelt and prayed by her bed. Emma, who later said that Nelson said goodbye to/her four times, and said he did not want to go, but that she urged him, and he said, 'Brave Emma. If there were more Emmas there would be more Nelsons', may have been exaggerating a little. She was, at this parting, so near a state of collapse that she could not go to the door where the post-chaise was waiting. It was Mr Matcham who saw Nelson off from Merton, and his subsequent behaviour tends to show that in that last, tense moment, Nelson confided Horatia to his care.

It was afterward remarked by several people that Horatia Nelson was serious, old for her age. Such a maturity may have stemmed from that time when she went to bed, blissfully ignorant, happy and secure, with a doting father within arm's reach, and woke to find him gone; gone, as it proved, forever. She was a month away from her official fifth birthday, in fact four years and eight months old, of an age to feel without much power to express her feelings.

Emma wept a great deal, but an upsurge of hope, natural to her,

followed the dead misery. She went to stay at Canturbury again and is said to have sung heartily with the choir in the anthem, 'My song shall be of Mercy and Judgement'. She also offered to sing at a charity concert but the offer was declined. Possibly her hopefulness and confidence were simulated, for after her return to Merton in October she suffered an attack of the nervous rash, severe enough to keep her in bed.

Cecilia Connor was acting as governess to Horatia at the time, and seems to have had considerable talent for teaching; the child was beginning to read. 'We read about twenty times a day as I do not wish to confine her long at a time.' Cecilia guided Horatia's hand when she attempted to write, and then Horatia pretended to guide hers; they played with dolls together; any effort at learning, any specially good behaviour was rewarded with kisses. Charlotte Nelson was there too, kind and attentive, and Mrs Cadogan was a doting grandmother. Surrounded by so much love, the child would hardly notice something missing in her mother's attitude toward her, and indeed Emma was no more casual than most mothers at the time. She was skilled enough in the art of pleasing to write warmly of Horatia to Nelson. 'What a blessing for her parents to have such a child, so sweet, altho' so young, so amiable.' That letter never reached Nelson, had it done it would have gone the way of all the others. Behaviour, however, counts for more than words, and at a time when many women, worried about a beloved man, would have sought some consolation in the company of his child, Emma did not. Horatia was left at Merton in the care of others, just as she had been left with Mrs Gibson. Emma's maternal instinct had been smothered long ago, and nothing in the circumstances of Horatia's conception, gestation and birth held very happy memories. There may also have been that unadmitted jealousy. There must have been some reason why Emma, always so kind, was capable of treating her own child with indifference and later with positive lack of kindness.

Nelson had more than once written letters to Horatia, knowing that they would be read to her; and with Cecilia Connor guiding

(opposite) After twenty-five days leave at Merton, Nelson left on the evening of the 13th of September to embark on the *Victory* at Portsmouth. Detail from *Farewell to Nelson* by A. C. Gow.

her hand, Horatia had written to him. On the 19th of October, kneeling at his desk in the *Victory* – kneeling because the ship was being cleared for action and his chair and his picture of Emma and his picture of Horatia had been taken below for safe keeping – he wrote a last letter to his daughter;

> My Dearest Angel, I was made happy by the pleasure of receiving your letter . . . and I rejoice to hear that you are so very good a girl and love my Dear Lady Hamilton who most dearly loves you, give her a kiss for me. The Combined Fleets of the Enemy are now reported to be coming out of Cadiz and therefore I answer your letter, my dearest Horatia, to mark to you that you are ever uppermost in my thoughts . . .

He admonished her to be a good girl and to pray for his safety, a conquest and a speedy return to dear Merton.

He then wrote to Emma, addressing her as 'My dearest beloved Emma, the dear friend of my bosom.' He mentioned the movements of the enemy, and the state of the weather. 'We have very little wind, so that I have no hopes of seeing them before to-morrow.' He added to that letter on the next day and that memorable word Trafalgar is mentioned for the first time. He ended, 'May God Almighty give us success over these fellows and enable us to get a peace.'

(left) Nelson wrote his last letter to Emma, kneeling at his desk on board the *Victory* on the eve of the Battle of Trafalgar, 19th of October 1805. (Egerton MS 1614, f. 125v.)

(opposite) Turner's painting of the Battle of Trafalgar was completed in 1806. He was much moved by the news of Nelson's death at Trafalgar and went to sketch the *Victory's* battle damage when she docked at Sheerness.

That was his last letter. After that he wrote only in a pocket-book journal. In it he wrote much as Emma wrote in her Memorials, listing the services she had done to her country and which he knew about.

> Could I have rewarded those services, I would not now call upon my Country, but as that has not been in my power, I leave Lady Emma Hamilton, therefore, a Legacy to my King and Country, that they will give her an ample provision to maintain her rank in life. I also leave to the benefice of my Country my adopted daughter, Horatia Nelson Thompson, and I desire She will use in future the name of Nelson only. These are the only favours I ask of my King and Country at this moment when I am going to fight their Battle . . . .

The valedictory note is not unusual though the vast majority of men go into action with the certainty that the bullet will hit the nextdoor fellow. But for that certainty, every fighting man would be a potential suicide.

Was Nelson one?

His health had not improved with age. His sight was failing, so were his lungs and he had suffered several heart attacks, which

at their peak he thought might kill him, and then when they had passed, were dismissed as spasms. He had achieved his ambition – to become a hero in the service of his country, he was beloved by every man who ever served under him, but he had never regarded himself as being adequately rewarded. He once said bitterly that other people had the rewards, 'poor Nelson all the hard knocks'. His leave at Merton had been happy, but there were flaws; the need to pretend that Horatia was adopted, and that he and Emma were not cohabiting. He must have asked himself if such subterfuges could be kept up forever. So sensitive a man might have been aware of the latent jealousy and imagined it worsening as Horatia grew up and Emma aged. His finances were hopelessly complicated. Compared with other problems, this may sound trivial, but it is on record that all the people who drowned themselves in one reach of the Thames over a period of years for whatever apparent reason, had one thing in common – they were penniless. In a low moment, having consigned Emma and Horatia

(opposite) The Death of Admiral Lord Nelson in the Moment of Victory, by Gillray. Emma appears as the woebegone Britannia.
(right) Captain Hardy, Nelson's lifelong friend, was to remain a friend to Emma. He urged Nelson, unsuccessfully, to change into a less conspicuous coat, and was with him when he died.

to the care of his country, he may have felt that he was of more worth to them dead than alive.

Otherwise why did he, the man the French feared above all others, deliberately make himself an obvious target by going into action wearing every decoration he possessed? England had lately been sparing with medals and ribbons but other countries had been generous. Turkey, in addition to the Plume of Triumph had sent the insignia of an Order which did not exist; informed, the Sultan hastily created the Order, with Nelson as its first member.

Hardy saw the decorations winking and shining and realized that for Nelson to wear them was tantamount to saying; I am Nelson; shoot me! He suggested a change of coat, and Nelson said there was no time for that. How long would such a change have taken? He had time enough to go around the ship and have a word with every man and boy aboard; a cheerful, confident word, despite one ill omen that morning.

Nelson was a religious man and superstition can be religion's near neighbour. Before each of his great victories a white bird had come and perched on the rigging of his ship. He had seen it himself, it had been seen by others. There was no white bird today. And when Nelson took leave of one of his captains he said, 'God bless you, Blackwood, I shall never speak to you again.'

The fatal shot broke his spine at about midday; and that he was aware of those betraying medals is shown by the fact that as he was being carried below to the shambles of a cockpit, he had them, as well as his face covered by a handkerchief, lest he should be recognized and his men lose heart. A handkerchief over the glittering show a little earlier might have saved his life.

The Nation Mourns

Remember that I leave Lady
Hamilton and my daughter to
my country.

Nelson, when dying

The tremendous victory was won on the 21st of October, positive
news reached London on the 6th of November, and at Merton,
Emma and Mrs Bolton who was staying with her, heard the bells
from the Tower of London. Mrs Bolton thought it might be news
from her brother; Emma thought it too early. And then a carriage
arrived bringing Captain Whitby with a letter from the Comp-
troller of the Admiralty. Even in this glorious and tragic moment,
protocol was observed; the First Lord of the Admiralty wrote only
to Fanny. Captain Whitby tried to cushion the blow by beginning,
'We have gained a great victory . . .' but he was so pale, so near
tears that the news he had come to convey needed no words.
Emma screamed and fell senseless.

When she recovered consciousness, even those not well-
disposed towards her said that she looked stunned, as though
unable to understand her loss. When she asked, as she did
repeatedly; What shall I do? How can I live? she was not, as
some supposed, concerned with money; she meant what could

(*previous page*) On the 8th of January 1806, the first day of Nelson's funeral, his
body was borne up river from Greenwich to Whitehall escorted by gun boats and
state barges. With jubilation and mourning interlinked England celebrated the
victory and death of her hero.

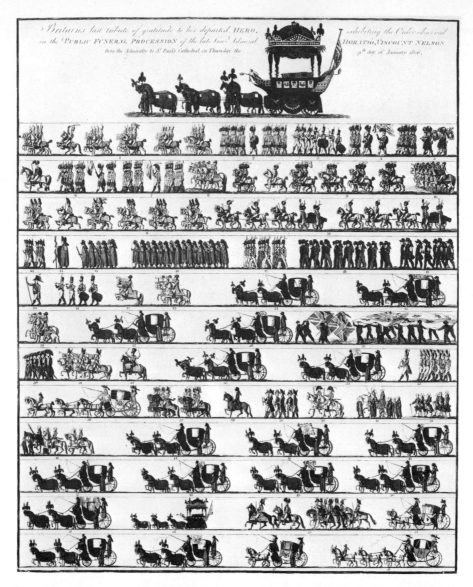

The order of the magnificent funeral procession from the Admiralty to St Paul's on the second day of Nelson's funeral.

she do, how could she live without the great love of her life. She said herself, 'my heart and head are gone'.

She had been gifted with beauty, talent, charm, a certain craftiness, even with that indefinable thing known as personality; but she lacked those inner resources which in the end are the only ones. She was like some exquisite, exotic, scented climbing plant which needs something about which to twine itself. She had depended utterly on that dry stump, Greville and when he threw her to the ground, had struggled up, not quite the same, but still

lively, to support herself on social success and political activity, devoting her energy to being a good wife to Sir William, a more-than-good friend to Maria Carolina, and a patriot to England. Then for seven years she had centred herself about Nelson, the best of all. 'I lived but for him. His glory I gloried in; it was my pride that he should go forth; and this fatal and last time he went I persuaded him to it. But I cannot go on . . .'

She was obliged to go on; she was only forty, and apart from the nervous rash, had good health. She was facing that hurdle in female life – the menopause – which has curious effects on level-headed, happily situated women. And she was obliged to stand by and watch helplessly while everything that Nelson had earned went to his brother William.

While England celebrated two conflicting events, the victory of Trafalgar and the death of Nelson, jubilation and mourning interlinked, the Government scattered a golden shower and further honours on his brother. Nelson had died a viscount, and poor, William was made an earl, Horace, now seventeen, a viscount; the earldom brought an allowance of £5,000 a year, and the grateful nation made a grant of £90,000 so that the new earl could buy an estate suitable to his rank. Golden drops fell elsewhere; each of Nelson's sisters received £15,000, Fanny had a pension of £2,000. For the hero's mistress and child, there was nothing.

It is impossible not to suspect – as Nelson himself had often done – something malignant working behind the scenes. Did this extraordinary generosity towards everybody else soothe a conscience somewhere?

Even at this distance of time one feels the sharp irony. William Nelson had done nothing, except, in Figaro's words, go to the trouble to get himself born, but he must have a fine estate; Nelson's beloved Merton, the poor low place, bought by instal-ments, was still deeply in debt for the improvements which had made it fit for a modest man's home.

The William Nelsons had been the first to desert Fanny and accept Emma in order to keep in with the famous man who might wield influence; they were the first to change sides. Charlotte was hastily called home. The Earl wrote a would-be ingratiating

(opposite) Nelson's funeral car reaches St Paul's.

letter to Fanny who had pride and dignity enough to ignore it. The Boltons and Matchams remained friendly with Emma; they liked her and loved Horatia but there is no evidence that either family gave her monetary assistance.

At first, and on the face of it, there was no need. She had £800 a year from Sir William's estate; Nelson had left her £2,000 as a gift, and an annuity of £500 to be paid out of his Bronte revenue; she would also control the income, about £200 a year, from Horatia's legacy: Merton and its original one-and-a-half acres was hers, so was the furniture there, and the furniture in the Clarges Street house. In theory she was comfortably placed. But the annuity from Bronte was fairy gold; Nelson had never received so much; he had employed two agents, neither honest; it was all too easy to shelter behind his expressed wish that the property should be improved and the peasants not squeezed. And a little later her Hamilton annuity was in jeopardy.

She had one asset – herself. She was forty and too plump, a very fullblown rose indeed; but there were men about who liked fullblown roses, men who would have been pleased and flattered to have as mistress, if not wife, the woman about whom so much scandal had centred for so many years; mistress to Greville, mistress to Sir William Hamilton, then Lady Hamilton, then mistress to the national hero. But, as she said, her heart was broken and life was not worth having. Grief and grievances could be temporarily forgotten in hard drinking and hard gambling; both one-way roads.

She still had friends; many naval officers who saw her touched with Nelson's glamour. Hardy was one; he had heartily deplored the whole business, but Nelson's last words had shown him how much Lady Hamilton meant to him. At Merton she had good neighbours, presently to prove their worth. She had goodwill from people she had never seen – Sir Walter Scott was one; their support took the form of believing that the Government should and would do something for her. Or perhaps the Earl, suddenly so

(opposite) A watercolour by Baxter of the Palladian porch and garden at Merton Place, Nelson's home in Surrey.
(overleaf) Death of Nelson by Dighton. He was shot in the spine at midday on the 21st of October during the Battle of Trafalgar, and died after hearing the news of the British victory.

rich would do something. Everybody waited for somebody else to do something.

There is some evidence that Emma's mind had broken with her heart. Whom was she deceiving when she wrote to the Earl that she did not know whether she would continue to live in England as she had promised the Queen of Naples to return there in case of accident? She knew very well that Maria Carolina had repudiated her. Similar excursions into fantasy were to crop up in the coming years, particularly in her Memorials which she continued to prepare and present.

The Earl had shown himself to be sycophantic, demanding, now he became positively greedy. Merton, he said, was divisible and the land on either side which Nelson had bought to ensure privacy and to enhance his home, must be sold to pay off the remaining mortgages and to provide for a number of small legacies left in Nelson's will. Such a division reduced Merton's desirability as a gentleman's residence, and Emma's improvements – many still unpaid for – had made the place unsuitable as anything else.

In 1806 there was another scandal, which naturally revived the others. Little Emma, now aged twenty-four, arrived in London claiming to be Emma's daughter. She shared the family fondness for name-changing, and now called herself Anne Carew. After old Mrs Kidd's death she had gone to live with the Connor family, but though the Connor girls had always been welcome at Merton after Sir William's death, Little Emma had never been invited. She had been well-educated, and held posts as governess.

Emma repudiated her absolutely and said that she was mad; that there was madness in the Connor family. The latter statement was true. Nelson had done his best to help Emma's family and had taken Charles Connor to sea with him, but the poor young man had gone demented and finally been classed as a dangerous lunatic. But the relationship between the Connors and Anne Carew or Emma Hart, or correctly, Emma Lyon was very slight indeed and the young woman was not mad. What prompted her to come to London cannot be known; she, like many others, may have regarded Emma as well-to-do and hoped to find with her

(opposite) Horatia Nelson dancing with a tambourine. Her pose is reminiscent of Emma's Attitudes, while the pendant around her neck bears a portrait of Nelson.

(left) Although Nelson's family gave Emma little financial aid some of her old friends did. This IOU is for the £500 sent her by Sir Harry Featherstonhaugh in July 1806.

(inset opposite) The 'wicked old' Duke of Queensberry, a disreputable millionaire, who even at eighty was an admirer of Emma's. He finally died in 1810, leaving Emma £500 a year – not as much as she had hoped.

a more pleasant life than that of a governess – notoriously ill-rewarded and socially awkward; she may have felt that she had been neglected long enough; she may even have felt a desire – common enough to people in her position – to be recognized by a real parent. Rejected by Emma, she went abroad, probably as a governess, 'a painful employment', she called it. She did not trouble Emma again, but Emma remembered her with a kind of viciousness, even going so far as to explain in her will that 'Ann Connor who goes by the name of Carew, and tells many falsehoods', was not her daughter. The spite may have been engendered by the fact that Anne Carew's arrival in London and the consequent revival of scandal, coincided with the presentation of yet another Memorial.

The house at Clarges Street was now too expensive to maintain and Emma moved out into furnished accommodation. The ease with which such apartments could be found at that time amazes the late-twentieth-century mind. The father of that arbiter of fashion, Beau Brummel, having saved enough from his wages as valet and his tips, bought an apartment house and prospered sufficiently to be able to send his son to Eton and to buy him a commission in the army. Upper servants, good cooks, skilled valets, careful housekeepers often joined together to provide rooms, with good service, for people who for various reasons did not wish to keep their own establishments in London. Emma's first lodging was relatively inferior. It was in New Bond Street and she was obliged to share the drawing room – and therefore be

154

A view of Richmond with Heron Court in the background on the left – one of many properties belonging to the Duke of Queensberry. Thinking that Emma was unsuitably housed, he offered it to her at a fairly low rent.

155

on equitable social terms, with her landlady. Mrs Bolton thought this regrettable, and so did the wicked old Duke of Queensberry. Not that he wanted to have Emma alone for any licentious reason; he was eighty years old and past the age of dalliance; but he was a relative of Sir William Hamilton, had been proud to call Nelson his friend, and he had long admired Emma. He thought she was unsuitably housed, and presently did something about it. He could, of course, have married her; at eighty he was still a bachelor, and he was a millionaire, but even Emma's best friends and Nelson's family always regarded her friendship with Queensberry as strictly Platonic; they did hope, however, that he would leave her something in his will. Emma hoped that he would buy Merton, paying just enough for it to clear the debts and leave her with so little as £100 in ready money. She wrote him a really pitiable letter, calling him the only hope she had in this world. Like many very old, very rich men he was egocentric and power hungry; he did not buy Merton, he had all the properties he wanted, and one of them was a mansion, called Heron Court, at Richmond and this he offered to Emma, not as a gift, but at a fairly low rent. She accepted it.

At about the same time the Matchams ended their nomad life and settled in a pleasant property called Ashfold in Sussex. Catherine Matcham had always wanted a settled home – not too far from London – and her gift from the Government helped.

The Boltons were still at Cranwich, and both there and at Ashfold, Emma and Horatia were welcome. Horatia had never gone permanently to live in Clarges Street, nor in the hired lodgings; she had lived at Merton, and if she missed Charlotte of whom she was fond, she still had Cecilia and Mrs Cadogan.

Emma had been approached by a hack writer – not a very successful one – who wished to write Nelson's biography. She agreed to help him by sharing her own reminiscences, allowing him free access to her papers and by giving him financial support while the book was being written. It was published toward the end of 1806 and was the first, some say the worst, of its kind. The writer, James Harrison, wished to flatter his patroness, and did so by denigrating Fanny, sometimes in terms which smack of dictation from Emma, and sometimes with a downright disregard for truth. Fanny may not have been the ideal wife for Nelson, but those who knew her knew that she had faced the break-up of her apparently happy marriage with great dignity and tolerance. It was absurd of Harrison, in an effort to please Emma to show Fanny as a fool who thought that the honours and wealth bestowed upon William Nelson should have gone to her son, Josiah Nisbet. Fanny was a sophisticated woman, she knew the rules that governed inheritances. A book too violently biased in favour of one woman at the expense of the other, naturally failed in its objective; it had a great deal of publicity, generally bad. It sold, of course, but considering Harrison's later behaviour it is doubtful if Emma benefitted much financially and her prestige suffered. Later, her association with Harrison did her irreparable damage.

After Queenberry's refusal to buy Merton it went on the market and was valued at £12,920. Somebody offered £13,000 for it, with all it contained; and then hastily withdrew. There was a question as to whether Emma had the right to sell it; for she had raised loans on it, just as she had raised loans on both her annuities.

The Matchams and the Boltons never quite understood why she wanted to rid herself of Merton, it was Nelson's special place, and to most things connected with him she held on grimly. Even the coat he had worn at Trafalgar with the blood around the hole

The bloodstained breeches and socks worn by Nelson at Trafalgar. Emma held on grimly to everything connected with her lover.

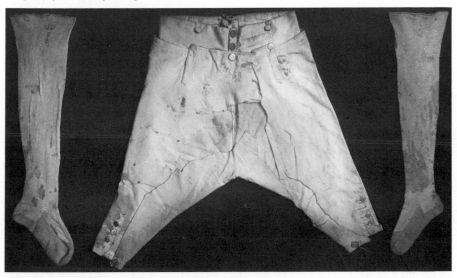

which the bullet had made, was carefully preserved. Why not his home, the only home he had ever owned, the place where he, and everybody else had been so happy? Perhaps the memories there were too poignant, too closely concerned with the living man, not like the rotting jacket, with the dead. And in any case she could not afford to keep Merton; what with borrowing, paying extortionate interest, and, quite possibly, some blackmail money, she was knee-deep in debt. At a public auction when Merton was put up for sale, there were no bidders. But friends and neighbours set up a formal trust, contributing sums which ranged from £1,000 to £200. Such a Trust could buy Merton, with all its debts and wait for the right moment to sell (Any believer in the theory that places as well as people have a destiny, might consider Merton with an eye to good luck or bad. When Emma bought it, it was plainly a farmhouse which for some reason had lost its land, and its outbuildings. It was briefly resurrected, but Nelson went out from it to die; one of the prime movers in its salvage in 1808 committed suicide when his banking firm faced ruin, and another suffered severe losses.)

Most of the gentlemen who came to Emma's rescue over Merton were shrewd business men; at the back of their friendly philanthropy they may have entertained the hope that in due time the Nation might buy Nelson's home and preserve it as a memorial. The idea never occurred. As usual the hero's modest homely side was overlooked and the enormous column went up in Trafalgar Square. It was unveiled – without the lions – in 1844, and just two years later Merton was demolished. The rooms which Emma had beautified, the garden she had made, the lawn on which Nelson had played with Horatia, the stream where Sir William had fished, even the pretty rustic bridge all vanished and the site was built over.

Three of Nelson's nephews were at Cambridge together; Lord Trafalgar, Tom Bolton and George Matcham. They moved in different sets. George Matcham wrote that he had seen Horace once, and no more, but that he saw Tom Bolton often. In an age of great snobbery there was nothing extraordinary in this, and to set against it was Horace's extreme love for and care for his pets. He was, however, hardly the young man to have fulfilled Nelson's hope that he would marry Horatia, a girl of unknown parentage,

The design for Nelson's column to be erected in Trafalgar Square. It was unveiled with some modifications, and without the lions, in 1844.

and very modest fortune. In the end he fulfilled nobody's hopes; in January 1808 he fell ill with what proved to be typhoid fever. He died after a few days and was buried in St Paul's Cathedral, near his famous uncle. Modest Tom Bolton moved a step nearer the earldom, and the Earl mingled his grief with resentment. His wife was now past the age for child-bearing. She lived another twenty years, but when she died he remarried, rather hastily. He was seventy-one, yet confident that with a young wife he might yet breed a son and scotch the Boltons' hopes. In this he was disappointed.

The Boltons, long before the Countess died and the second marriage was made, had assumed that Tom would become the second Earl, and began looking around for a more suitable home than the farm at Cranwich. The lease was about to run out and on the whole it had been an unrewarding enterprise. They eventually found Bradenham Hall in Norfolk, and moved there in 1811.

Emma had meantime taken up residence at Heron Court and after the rather mean, cramped London lodgings – quite unsuitable for Horatia – the mansion by the Thames seemed wonderful. The change went to her head; she began to entertain again in lavish style. Word got about and all her creditors were naturally annoyed, thinking that if she could live in a mansion and give parties, she might consider her debts. They began to press for payment and Emma pursued her rake's progress, paying a little here and there when she could, stalling off the more importunate, opening fresh accounts with trusting people impressed by her name and her Heron Court address.

Horatia went to Richmond, and the move must have been a watershed in her young life. It meant saying goodbye to Merton where she had been so happy; it meant regular, daily association with her mother, whom she had been taught to adore, and who had been, at a distance, or during brief contacts, adorable. They were too much alike in some ways; both highly strung, both subject to that nervous rash – a fact which, had it been noted, would have given a clue to their real relationship. Emma's temper had always been unreliable, worry and drink had not improved it. Nelson, too, for all his good nature, had been easily irritated, so with the move to Richmond two potentially explosive elements had been brought together. Nelson, however, had possessed great self control, and an overriding sense of duty; these Horatia had inherited together with the easily exasperated nerves; she developed an enormous, precocious self-control and an enormous, precocious sense of duty towards the woman who was her godmother and guardian, the woman whom her adored father had loved.

That Emma was her mother, Horatia could not have guessed. Mrs Cadogan and Emma had kept the secret so well that even Nelson's early biographers – more serious than James Harrison – assumed the existence of another woman in Nelson's life, some mistress before Emma. And Emma herself, indulging a flight of fancy, dropped hints that Horatia was actually the daughter of the Queen of Naples. On this story Horatia, years later, made cogent comment; she called it 'most incredible – had it been so, of course I should have passed as her husband's child.' By that time she knew her world and knew that all Maria Carolina's sixteen children had been acknowledged by Ferdinand.

In moving to Richmond, Horatia had lost more than Merton; Cecilia Connor was replaced by a French governess. Emma was not alone in confusing education with accomplishments, but Horatia's letters at the age of fourteen rather suggest, considering how quickly and easily she had learned to read and write, that she would have done better had Cecilia remained in charge of at least the basic lessons. When Cecilia left she was owed thirty pounds and joined Emma's other creditors in dunning her.

Emma spoke often of the need for economy and of making ends meet, but she never managed it and one reason is made plain by what George Matcham, observant and critical as ever wrote after he had visited Heron Court on his way back to Cambridge.

> . . . alas! how different was that table now to what I had before been accustomed; where formerly elegance presided, vulgarity and grossièreté was now introduced. I could almost have wept at the change. A plan of economy has been most laudably laid down by her Ladyship but I could have wished that the crowd of obsequious attendance had been entirely dismissed, instead of being partially diminished.

To deny that Emma had a vulgar streak would be to diminish her achievement in making herself acceptable to so many un-vulgar people; she could always fit her behaviour to her company, and she now felt the positive need for 'obsequious attendance'. The treatment she had received had made her paranoic; she could tolerate only people who praised and flattered her, as they gorged her food and drank her wine. Eating and drinking with them, accepting their flattery, she could forget, if only briefly, that her beauty had departed, that she was ageing and fat, worried about money and ignored by the Government who owed her so much.

Drinking immoderately as an escape from grief and grievance was relatively new to her. Sir William would never have tolerated it; and Nelson was noted for his abstemiousness. He was not often with her, but she loved him enough to be influenced by his example. And in the early stages at least, she could control her drinking; otherwise she would not have been welcome at Ashfold and Cranwich. She could still have been saved both financially and psychologically, by a stroke of good fortune; a little re-cognition of her services, a small pension from the Government to whom Nelson had left her as a legacy. As it was, everything conspired against her.

She was self-indulgent, over-generous, extravagant, and floundered from one monetary crisis to another. The possibility of her being blackmailed should be considered, for as an eroder of financial stability the blackmailer takes first place. Not in her immediate entourage, but in the background was a rather sinister character called Olivier.

He had joined Sir William's household as a boy, employed in a menial capacity, and stayed in his employ until he died. Emma had then dismissed him, and he had become her enemy. He was a friend of James Harrison, and while the *Life of Nelson*, that book which so many found disgusting, was being prepared, Olivier had supplied some intimate details which could not be used just then because the purpose of the book was to exalt Lady Hamilton. Olivier was a liar; he told Harrison that he had joined Sir William as courier and linguist during the homeward journey in 1800; but liar or not, he obviously *knew* something. After Emma was dead he collaborated with an anonymous writer who compiled the *Memoirs of Lady Hamilton*. In it Olivier claimed to have gone with Emma to take the baby to Mrs Gibson. It was highly unlikely that he did so. Emma was a gambler, but she would not have taken such a risk; and if he had been there, Mrs Gibson's daughter, Jane, thirteen at the time, would have remembered him. Asked, years later, when Horatia was anxious to know what was to be known, Jane Gibson stated categorically that Lady Hamilton had come unattended. But for a sharp-witted young man it would not have been difficult to make a connection between Lady Hamilton, grossly fat, taking to her bed and after an interval getting up, much thinner, and then taking a sudden, intense interest in a boarded-out baby. Olivier, if he wished to blackmail Emma, knew enough to exert pressure on the most sensitive spot of all; and what he knew could be added to what James Harrison knew because he read Nelson's letters, and later, Emma always said, stole some of them.

By autumn of 1809, Emma realized that she could not afford to live at Richmond any longer; a place of that size, however cheaply rented, needed upkeep and staff beyond her means. She, Horatia and Mrs Cadogan went back to London, this time not to an apartment of any kind, but to plain hired lodgings, frequently changed and growing worse with each move. For the first time since her brief stay at Up Park, there is some mystery about her exact whereabouts. She may have been dodging creditors. Once she gave her address as 36 Albemarle Street, but young Lady Bolton called there and nobody knew anything of Lady Hamilton; even a postman had never heard of her.

What is known is that in London everybody became ill.

Horatia's ailment was never diagnosed; Mrs Cadogan suffered from bronchitis; Emma had trouble with her liver.

Mrs Cadogan had for some years been bronchial, always preferring country air; now she was breathing London fog; she had always been a good, careful housekeeper, ruling Greville's dainty house, and the Palazzo Sessa, and Merton, and Heron Court, differing places, in differing circumstances, as well as she could; now she was hampered and constricted. There can be no doubt that Emma's declining fortunes depressed and alarmed her; she had seen Emma rise, and now to see her fall must have been painful. The change in the company she kept would not have gone unnoticed – it was Mrs Cadogan who had deplored the behaviour of the old Kidd relative.

Mrs Cadogan died in the bleak January of 1810 and was buried in the churchyard at Paddington Green, not far from the house where she and Emma had lived with Greville.

In Sir William Emma had lost a husband and a friend; in Nelson a lover; in her mother she lost the one person who knew all about her, the one before whom no attitude was needed. There had been absolute confidence between them, in good days and bad. Soon Emma was to be reproaching Horatia for not being as good a daughter as she herself had been – while at the same time she denied that Horatia was her daughter, a typical inconsistency.

About her mourning for Sir William there was a touch of perfunctoriness; Nelson she had mourned sincerely, but with more than a touch of drama. Mrs Cadogan was mourned with raw sorrow. She was irreplaceable. (Once a King of England, coming back from Crusade was greeted in Sicily with the news that his two young sons were dead. A little later he was told his father was dead. The King of Sicily asked why the second piece of information upset him more and he replied that a man could have other sons, never another father.)

Horatia's loss was serious, too; she had lost not only a loving grandmother, but another piece of her stable background. And this year, though repeatedly invited to go to Cranwich, Emma did not do so, Horatia was therefore cut off from her Bolton cousins of whom she was fond. Life narrowed down to mean lodgings over a confectioner's shop and the company of an often irritable guardian, and the hope that when the Duke of Queensberry died he would leave Lady Hamilton a handsome legacy. Even Mrs

Bolton shared that hope and attributed Emma's non-acceptance of her invitations to Emma's wish to keep in with the old man; '. . . for, depend upon it. Whoever is most in favor will then have the Largest Legacy.'

The need for money was now desperate. Charles Greville had died in 1809 and all that he owned – including what he had inherited from Sir William, passed to his brother, Fulke Greville who made the settlement of the estate an excuse for suspending Emma's £800 a year. She had already borrowed – and spent, money loaned on her anticipations.

Queensberry died at last, in December 1810 and he had re-membered Lady Hamilton in his will. Not handsomely, considering how much he had professed to admire her and value her friendship, and the fact that he was so very wealthy, but £500 a year, paid regularly, could have been something of a lifebuoy.

As soon as the terms of the will were known, Emma moved to better lodgings at 16 Dover Street; and there she received two cautionary letters. One from Mrs Matcham who added to her congratulations, the sober words, 'with economy it will enable you to live comfortably'. The other, from one of the trustees of the Hamilton estate was more explicit. 'I hope you never an-ticipate the quarter you *expect to* become due . . . you should be *cautious* not to increase your expenditure till your affairs *are settled* or your creditors will become very troublesome . . .'

They were troublesome already and became more so, especially when it was known that Queensberry's will was being generally contested and it might be years before Emma received a penny. In April Emma was obliged to beg the loan of £100 from Mr Matcham, who lent it so readily and with such confidence, 'I know you will repay it as soon as you can', that he could not have understood her true situation. It would be typical of her to spend some of this loan on a party to celebrate her forty-sixth birthday at the Ship Inn near Greenwich Park. She was seen making her way there, with the one Connor, Sarah, with whom she was still on speaking terms, Horatia and several other children. The gentleman, who had known her in Palermo, obviously recognized her, but she looked so slovenly, with a shawl just thrown over her head, that he hesitated to speak to her. However, that she was still capable of making a decent appearance was proved later on, in December of the same year when she made her last visit to

The Ship Inn, Greenwich, where Emma went slovenly dressed and with only a shawl thrown over her head to spend part of Mr Matcham's loan of £100 on a party to celebrate her forty-sixth birthday.

Norfolk. The Boltons had three things to celebrate, the house-warming at Bradenham Hall into which they had just moved, Christmas, and then two days later, the marriage of Eliza Bolton to a cousin, Henry Girdlestone. She could not have looked slovenly then for she was treated as the guest of honour and asked to sign the parish register as a witness. And with so much to celebrate some degree of inebriation would pass unnoticed. That was the last family gathering for Emma, for Horatia the last for some time.

CHAPTER
9

Within the Rules

I ask not anything but right
and to know weather I am to
receive my due or not?

Emma to Earl Nelson

One way to evade creditors was to keep on the move, and Emma and Horatia spent 1812 changing lodgings; often the Matchams and Boltons did not know where she was; letters remained unanswered, invitations ignored. They still had no true conception of her circumstances; a letter from one of the Bolton girls to Horatia expressed the hope that another visit to Bradenham might take place, 'as soon as the gaieties of London permit you'.

With the New Year, 1813, Emma had at least a fixed address, she and Horatia were in the King's Bench prison for debt.

Committing people – sometimes whole families – to gaol because of nonpayment of bills, appears on the face of it to be a futile exercise. A person unable to meet his obligations while living in his own home did not become magically endowed with the power to do so when shut away behind prison walls; but the custom served two practical purposes. The prospect of being gaoled made people willing to beg, borrow or steal in order to avoid incarceration, prisons were not pleasant places; and if a person were gaoled, his relatives and friends used every effort and resource to get him out.

(previous page) With the New Year 1813, Emma had at least a fixed address. She and Horatia were in the King's Bench prison for debt.

168

Female debtors were rare since fathers were responsible for unmarried girls, and husbands for their wives; only reckless spinsters of full age and spendthrift widows were held responsible for their debts; the curious legal situation was made perfectly clear over the interesting case concerning a young woman's expensive trousseau; her father denied all responsibility because she was now a married woman, her husband refused to pay because the expense was incurred before she was his wife. Faced with such a deadlock there was little that an honest supplier of goods could do, except keep quiet and tack a little on to the bills of those able and willing to pay. Emma, Lady Hamilton, was responsible for her own debts, and could be arrested and held, until they were discharged.

But she was spared the worst. Even among debtors there were graduations. The poor and totally obscure might go to rot and sicken inside the walls; more privileged people, those with titles, with powerful friends, lived 'within the rules'. Adjacent to debtors' gaols, outside the prison walls but within a limited area, there were the sponging houses in which the privileged debtor could live in no great discomfort, and at considerable expense, limited as to movement, but allowed visitors, allowed to buy, or to accept gifts of, food. The keepers of the sponging houses provided as little and exacted as much as they could and conditions were naturally squalid.

As soon as the Boltons and the Matchams knew where Emma was, they acted, but not exactly in the way that the creditors, and perhaps Emma herself had hoped. The Boltons sent food; the Matchams urged that Horatia should be sent to Ashfold, where they would regard her as one of their own. Most women in Emma's position would have snatched at a chance to get Horatia away from such surroundings and from such company as a sponging house held, but Emma hung on to Horatia because she had come to regard her as an asset. Her own claims and Memorials had come to nothing, but she still hoped that something would be done for Nelson's daughter, and felt that while she had the girl in her guardianship she herself amounted to something. It was not a maternal attitude and is less to her credit than many other things she did or failed to do. In a way it was a measure of how far her character had deteriorated. She may have been oblivious to some of the sights and sounds and forgotten that Horatia was young, the product of a sheltered childhood.

One of the neighbours at Merton, one of those who had helped form the Trust to relieve her of it, was Mr Perry, editor of the *Morning Chronicle*. He had proved to be a reliable friend; often when other papers were hostile, the *Morning Chronicle* had defended her. From the sponging house she appealed to him and he acted quickly, helped by an influential Alderman of the City, Mr Smith.

Her affairs were muddled almost beyond comprehension; her Hamilton annuity was pledged for years ahead, and she had already sold some things – the silver-gilt cup which Nelson had given Horatia, for example. Somehow Mr Perry and Mr Smith raised enough money, not to clear her debts, but to bail her out of the King's Bench precincts, and in mid-February she was back in Bond Street, busy with the completion of two more Memorials doomed to be, if possible, more ill-fated than their predecessors. In one she told a blatant lie, saying that Mr Canning had told Nelson in the presence of a witness that her claim on the Government was valid and should be met. Such a lie was easily exposed, Canning denied it, and the witness said he had never been present at a meeting where such an assurance was given.

The other petition was addressed to the Prince Regent, formerly Prince of Wales. The poor old King's mind had finally failed altogether and Emma was hopeful that an appeal to this erstwhile admirer might have results. But princes change their minds, especially after they come to power, and there was another thing working against Emma. Nelson's letters. The book was not yet published, but it was in the process of preparation, and was the kind of book to be talked about beforehand. Some rumour of the opinion Nelson had held of him must have reached the Prince's ears. Lord Sidmouth, writing for the Prince Regent made it painfully clear that Emma had nothing to hope for, and at the same time Lord Liverpool said to Nelson's solicitor that, 'nothing could be done for Miss Nelson while she remained under Lady Hamilton's roof'.

Emma always denied that she had either sold the letters to Harrison, or given him permission to make use of them. She had allowed him access to them while he wrote his earlier book, praising her so highly, denigrating Fanny. Toward the end, as her reckless statement about Canning and Nelson showed, she no longer distinguished precisely between truth and fiction, but she was at least *unlikely* to have sold Harrison the letters or given him permission to print them unexpurgated. Some of them were altogether too revealing, exposing the true relationship between Nelson and herself, and exploding the Thompson myth.

When the book was advertised, early in 1814, the publishers said that the original letters were *in their possession*. The most probable explanation is her own, that they were stolen. And that she was blackmailed, 'pay or I publish'. By 1813 when she could no longer pay, preparations to publish went ahead.

When the book was published, Emma was back 'within the rules', this time at the Temple.

Mr Perry and Alderman Smith, in February 1813 had managed to obtain her only a temporary reprieve, and then followed it up by arranging for all her visible assets to be sold by auction.

Considering the peripatetic life she had lately led, she had managed to retain a considerable number of things, household goods, and relics of Nelson, the remnants of Sir William's library and a few pictures. Some had undoubtedly been hidden from her creditors in the house of her actress friend, Mrs Billington, but there is a strong supposition that during her wanderings she had let her house furnished. Now everything must go, even Horatia's doll's bedstead and the apparatus for games such as Draft Board and Men, all relics of happy days at Merton and of Cecilia Connor.

Alderman Smith spent £490 at the sale, but he also took some items as security against the money he had already spent on Emma – and money he was to spend in future. He had the articles crated and taken to his warehouse. Since he then made himself responsible for her expenses at the second sponging house, and even paid fifteen shillings a month on the hire of a piano for Horatia's benefit, and in the end cleared her debts and paid for her funeral, he must have lost heavily on the transaction.

This time Emma stayed within the rules for a year. A few of her creditors were still dissatisfied and demanded that she should remain there until they were paid. The rent of the rooms she occupied was three-and-a-half guineas a week, she had to buy coal if she wished for a fire and she had to buy her own food and liquor and pay a washerwoman. Most things brought in from without passed through the hands of the sponging-house keeper who took his cut; and his bill for breakages, over £13, would

When Alderman Smith obtained Emma a reprieve in February 1813, an auction was arranged in which all her visible assets were sold. Even her chatelaine and Nelson's snuffboxes would have gone.

seem excessive, unless, as Winifred Gerin suggests, Emma flung things when she was angry and drunk. Nelson's solicitor put it more mildly saying that there were times when Lady Hamilton was warm with wine and anger. Wine however was not her only beverage, nor was the relatively harmless porter; she had taken to spirits, which were very bad for her failing liver. She frequently felt ill and stayed in bed.

Horatia's life must have been unenviable. She and her mother were basically unsuited for life together. Emma frequently accused her of being ungrateful, of telling lies. She probably said more hurtful things, too. Mrs Cadogan when she was alive had been obliged to remonstrate with Emma about the language she used to the child. Horatia sometimes lost her temper, too, and there were acrimonious scenes, for which the girl was the first to apologize. She showed amazing stoicism and a devotion, all the more creditable because real affection was lacking and because she knew that there was no necessity for her to be in this horrible place at all – she could have been at Ashfold, with the Matchams. In later years Horatia's anxiety to know about her real parentage may have stemmed from a desire to know that Emma was *not* her mother. The pretty, sweet-scented, gaily-dressed Dear Lady who had flashed in and out of her childhood days had vanished into a drunken, raddled, slovenly old woman.

The Matchams knew where Emma was; they sent her potatoes, and promised a turkey for Christmas. They did not offer financial aid, though they had always been comfortably off and the Government had given Mrs Matcham £15,000. It may be that they believed that left in the sponging house long enough, Emma would come to her senses and let Horatia go. The tie with the Bolton family had loosened after the death of Mrs Bolton. Emma very seldom answered the letters from the Matchams; perhaps

Horatia's portrait painted in about 1815 shows that she had inherited Nelson's features rather than her mother's lovely face – possibly why she never believed herself to be Emma's daughter.

she thought they should have done more to help, perhaps she feared their plans to get Horatia away from her. Horatia wrote and received letters, and this may have angered Emma and made her smash things. There was, in fact nothing to prevent Horatia from simply leaving; she was not a debtor, she was free to come and go. She was sometimes invited to Alderman Smith's home; he had two daughters of about her age. He would have lent her the coach fare to Ashfold . . . Horatia seems to have inherited Nelson's strong sense of duty, and maybe, in the midst of the wreck that was Emma, the ghost of charm sometimes flickered . . .

Occasionally her zest for entertaining flickered too. She kept the anniversary of the Battle of the Nile by inviting Sir Thomas Lewis – apparently one of her few remaining acquaintances, and a priest – she sometimes had religious inclinations – and her doctor to come and drink to Nelson's immortal memory. 'He cou'd never have thought that his Child and myself shou'd pass the anniversary of that day were we shall pass it.'

Emma could sometimes choose her words well, and *immortal memory* was not an ill-judged phrase; to this day where men go down to the sea in ships, he is remembered. Navies at the time undreamed of were to wear a modification of the English sailors' dress, which incorporated mementoes of his three great victories, and of his death. And for decades, well into the twentieth century, the best dress for thousands of little boys, in many countries and of many classes, was a miniature copy of English sailors' wear. But the women whom he had adored and the child he had idolized, kept the anniversary with three friends in a sponging house attached to a debtors' gaol.

That was on the 1st of August; at Christmas that year Emma roused herself and gave another party, with rather more distinguished guests, one of whom, Sir William Dillon, wrote an

173

account of it. It gives an interesting sidelight upon life in a sponging house. He was the first guest to arrive and saw a table set for four and displaying a great deal of silver plate but a shortage of cutlery. The plate had been hired and those who supplied it had not foreseen the need for a carving knife and fork. Sir William, who had not seen Emma for three years and with whom she had renewed contact through the Admiralty, was surprised – one hopes pleasantly – to find that his fellow guests were His Royal Highness, the Duke of Sussex and his mistress, Mrs Bugge. Even the mistress of princes, unless they had social standing of their own, could not be 'received', in Society, and the Duke of Sussex must have been glad to take Mrs Bugge to some place – however dubious the address – where she would be accepted and entertained.

The first course, Sir William reported, went well, but when 'a good-sized bird', most likely the turkey from Ashfold, was placed on the table and Emma asked him to carve it, he complained that he had no implements. Emma said, 'Oh, you must not be particular here!' He was prepared to dismember the bird with his hands, saying jokingly that having been a midshipman he knew how to use his fingers. 'My reply produced some hearty laughter, and the repast terminated very merrily. After a sociable and agreeable entertainment, I took my leave'.

It is a pity that Horatia was not present to see how her mother could still rise to an occasion and resuscitate that *ambiance* of good fellowship and merriment which had once been one of her

His Royal Highness the Duke of Sussex, who with his mistress Mrs Bugge came to the last dinner party Emma gave, on Christmas Day 1813, in the sponging house. There was a good-sized bird and a great deal of hired silver plate, but no knives or forks.

gifts. The table was set for four; Horatia was spending a night at Alderman Smith's.

Emma was still living within the rules, when in April 1814, Napoleon abdicated and went into his first exile in Elba. England went mad with joy. This, people thought – a little prematurely – was peace at last and they celebrated it with illuminations and fireworks and processions and banquets and special shows in theatres, much as people in Palermo had celebrated the victory of the Nile. This time Emma had no part in it. Other voices were singing what had been her theme song – 'Rule Britannia'.

But Nelson was not forgotten, and into a country aglow with patriotic fervour the *Letters of Lord Nelson to Lady Hamilton* was launched, priced at a guinea.

Nelson had destroyed all her letters and had repeatedly urged her to destroy his and she had not done so. Here they were, for all to read. The cautious letters with Nelson masquerading as Thompson; the frank letters, when he was certain of direct delivery into her hand.

It was futile for her, having read the first advertisement of the book in the *Morning Herald*, to sit down and write an impassioned letter to Mr Perry of the *Morning Chronicle*, saying that on her honour she knew nothing of the letters. She meant of course that she knew nothing of their publication. She knew about the letters; she had received them, read them and kept them. After Nelson's death they had lain scattered upon her bed; then she had allowed Harrison to read some, if not all, of them. And then they had passed out of her possession and that she *must* have known. A bundle of letters of deep sentimental value – and potentially dangerous – does not simply vanish without the owner being aware of the fact. Writing to Perry, saying the letters might be 'the invention of a vile, mercenary wretch', mentioning where she was, how ill she had been and how there had once been a fire in her house and she had left her papers with a person she thought she could rely upon, all added up to the incoherent, rambling kind of letter which sensible editors do *not* publish. Even Mr Perry's good heart stopped short of that; if at that moment, Emma could have produced even *one* letter from Nelson which differed from the printed page, she would have had a case; as it was, she had none.

CHAPTER

10

Calais

Dear Lady, the bright day is
done and we are for the dark.

Iris to Cleopatra

The Allies, English, Prussian and Russian were in Paris, and
Louis XVIII, after a long and not-always-happy exile in England
was on his way to be crowned. France was again open to the
English, who had for years regarded it as the first stage of the
Grand Tour which formed part of a privileged Englishman's
education. Many people in the late spring and early summer of
that year were planning to go abroad, and the restless Mr Matcham was one of them. He had never been a debtor and he plainly
did not understand Emma's plight; he wrote that he and his family
were going abroad, destination unknown, some town or village
in the sun; and he invited Emma and Horatia to join him; his
carriage would be at her disposal anywhere, any time.

People living within the rules were sometimes allowed to take
little outings for the sake of their health; constricted rides, so far
and no farther, in carriages driven by approved coachmen, part
of the gaol-sponginghouse network. Emma knew, though Mr
Matcham obviously did not, that for her to get into his carriage
and drive off to an unknown destination, would be virtually

(previous page) A view of Calais in the early nineteenth century. Emma was
forced to spend the last few months of her life there in order to escape further
imprisonment for debt in England.

178

impossible, and, if possible, the equivalent of breaking out of gaol. Enticing as Mr Matcham's offer was, with the prospect of escape and *free* travel, it could not be accepted. But the idea of going abroad lodged in her mind and persisted. Only with the Channel between her and her creditors would she ever feel safe. Even if the three specific debts which had landed her here were paid off, others would be left, and the fact that sending her to prison had produced money from somewhere would encourage the remaining creditors to have her re-arrested.

However, to travel cost money and she had none; unwillingly she appealed to Earl Nelson. There is hardly a more striking or sadder contrast anywhere than between the arch, almost flirtations letters which had made a dull country parson feel like a man of the world and the one written by the same woman to the same man in April of 1814. Addressing him as 'My Lord', she began, 'It cannot be more disagreeable to you to Receive a Letter from me than it is for me to write to you.' She then asked him to send her *some* money out of what was due to her, under Nelson's will, from the Bronte estate. 'I ask not alms, I ask not anything but right and to know weather I am to receive my due or not.'

The Earl saw the force of that argument, for he promptly sent her £225, for which she sent a receipt and the assurance that this was not money pledged in advance. Had it been so he would have been in error in paying it to her, since it belonged to the money-lender who had made the loan.

She retained exactly £50 for her own use and sent the rest to Mr Perry and Alderman Smith who organized a collection for her in the City, added their contribution and paid all her immediate debts – tradesmen were paid, and in the last week in June, Lord Ellenborough discharged her. She was, for the moment, free. But sums far beyond anything that her City friends could provide were still owing to the moneylenders who had advanced loans on her expectations, at extortionate interest, so for fear of re-arrest she was obliged to move very secretly. (In the end the money-lenders were reimbursed, for they had taken the sensible precaution of insuring her life with the Pelican Insurance Company.) Emma dared not embark on the ordinary packet boat, which made the crossing in a day, but took a passage on a small, slow ship, the *Tom Thumb*, which left from London Bridge Wharf. She and Horatia went aboard after dark on the last night of June 1814.

In June 1814, Emma and Horatia fled to France in a small, slow ship, which left London Bridge Wharf near the Tower.

So, furtively, she departed from England, her England, the country of which she had been so proud and which she had served so well, and which had served her so badly.

Tom Thumb took three days to make the crossing, and both passengers were horribly seasick, but they survived and landed in Calais, which was crowded with English people bound for Paris, all agog to see the city where a King and a Queen had been beheaded by Dr Guillotine's merciful invention, and some streets had been so soaked with the blood of aristocrats that cattle, coming in to be slaughtered could not be forced to cross them.

Travel in those days was leisurely, if not easy; people who had made the Channel crossing needed a rest before taking to the road. So there were hotels in Calais, and the best was Dessein's, patronized by the richer English people. Emma now had less than

180

£50 – she had been obliged to pay fares – but she went to Dessein's. This was not quite the simple act of witless extravagance that it seemed. She wanted Horatia to be seen and admired; who knew? among fellow guests in such a place there might be some who would espouse their cause?

Hope made its final appearance. Horatia at thirteen was, if not pretty, very presentable. She was tall for her age, she had been trained in deportment, played several musical instruments with grace and adequacy, spoke French above average; and after the publication of the letters she was acknowledged as Nelson's daughter. Somebody must surely notice her. Hope showed another face, too; the Prince Regent in refusing to make an allowance had pleaded shortage of public funds; now the war was ended and everybody at Dessein's seemed to have plenty of money. Something must surely happen. Nothing did. The rich, the ones with power, might pay Horatia a compliment or two, then they moved on.

By August sheer shortage of ready money obliged Emma to move on, too, into the commune Saint-Pierre, a village two miles out of Calais, where she lodged in a farmhouse. Food was amazingly cheap; one could buy a turkey for the equivalent of two shillings, a brace of partridges for five pence, good wine for fifteen pence a bottle, inferior stuff for five.

But even the cheapest food, the humblest lodging, costs something and Emma was, she wrote herself, 'without a penny in her pocket'. Horatia's half-yearly interest on her legacy was not due until her supposed birthday on the 29th of October. One wonders, indeed, how they did live.

In September Emma appealed to Fulke Greville saying that he knew how long it was since she had been paid her annuity and asking him to send her £100. He sent a chilly reply; since her Hamilton annuity was mortgaged he must not venture to make any payments to her.

She wrote in early October to Lord Sidmouth, through whom her Memorial to the Prince Regent had been rejected. 'If there is Humanity still left in British Hearts they will not suffer us to die of famine in a foreign country for God's sake then send us some relief.' Nothing came of that. She wrote a private letter, complaining of the behaviour of Earl Nelson and all she said in it was true; Horace had been educated at Eton at Nelson's expense, she

The Departure of a French Diligence from a Courtyard by Rowlandson. On their arrival in France, Emma and Horatia went to Dessein's, the best posting inn in Calais, hoping that a rich English traveller might espouse their cause.

herself had helped to educate Charlotte, given her many presents, launched her into Society, used influence to get the Reverend William his prebendary stall at Canterbury. She wrote a public letter to the Editor of the *Morning Herald* which had gone so far as to say that she had skipped her bail. 'This is false; and I had had Ellenborough's discharge.' At the same time she took a chance to refer to the letters. 'Sir W. Hamilton, Ld N and myself were too much attached to his Royal Highness ever to speak or think ill of him. If I had the means I wou'd prosecute the wretches who have thus traduced me . . . I entreat you to contradict the falsehood concerning my bail and also the other malicious reports.' She signed herself, 'the much injured, Emma Hamilton.'

Generally she asked that replies to her letters should be addressed to Dessein's Hotel in Calais, and that was not pretentiousness. She must have felt the insecurity of her refuge at the famhouse, and hotels were accustomed to acting as *poste restante*. Horatia must have walked the two miles into Calais and back, for Emma was now incapable of much activity. She had an attack of jaundice, and was suffering from dropsy; neither complaint helped by her growing intemperance.

It was left for Horatia to do the begging. She wrote to Earl

Nelson, who sent a grudging £10 and to 'a kind friend', probably Alderman Smith, who sent £20. This money probably enabled Emma and Horatia to pay what they owed at Saint-Pierre and move into Calais, to one hired room at 27 Rue Française; it was the meanest lodging of all; Horatia slept in a kind of alcove, scooped

Lighthouse and Grande Place, Calais. In the autumn of 1814, Emma moved back from Saint-Pierre into the centre of Calais to live in one squalid room. She died there on the 15th of January 1815.

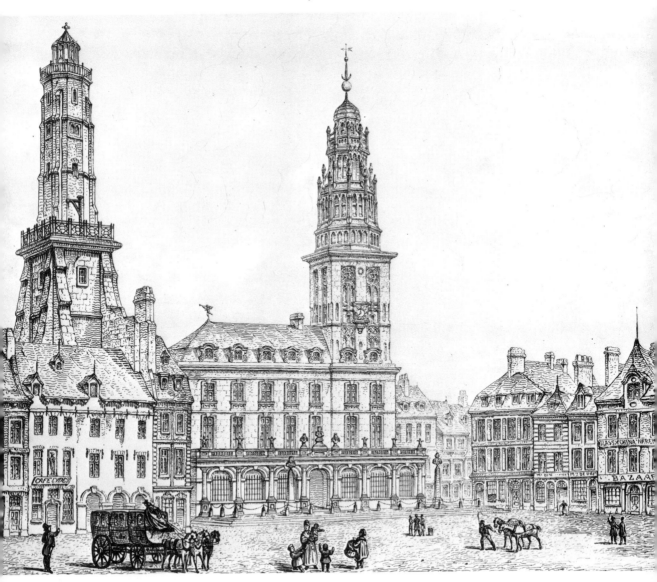

183

out of the wall. And now, instead of the walk into Calais in the hope of a letter waiting at the hotel, she walked to pawnshops. Anything of real value had long since been disposed of; only a few almost worthless trinkets and bits of wearing apparel remained to be pawned. There is mention of an Indian shawl, and it may have been one of those with which, in a different world, Emma had performed her Attitudes. It could even have been the one which, at Sir William's behest, she had thrown over her head and, adopting an attitude of prayer, reduced a priest to tears.

Horatia wrote to Mr Matcham. In the April he had been planning to go abroad and settle somewhere in the sun, but either his plans had gone wrong, or he had made a brief visit to the Continent and failed to find what he wanted. In any case he was still at Ashfold and Horatia's letter reached him. There is no evidence that he sent money; but he did most strongly urge her to come home as soon as she could find a reliable person to look after Lady Hamilton. He was a worthy man, but he must have been singularly obtuse. Where, in a foreign land and without money, could Horatia have found a reliable hireling?

Emma and Horatia were surrounded by strangers, and not particularly friendly ones. The French might put up an act of friendliness toward the rich English, dripping golden guineas in their wake, but the two countries had been at war, with one brief intermission, since 1792, and the French adored Napoleon rather more than the English adored Nelson. The English had – temporarily – defeated Napoleon, and though smiles might be forced, ready palms outstretched toward summer visitors, it was impossible that any true Frenchman should look kindly upon any English; least of all the paramour and the daughter of Nelson, reduced to penury.

Winter was settling in.

Even in summer, even now, even to the happy holiday maker, bound for the South, there is something desolate about Calais and the country immediately surrounding it, desolate and faintly inimicable to man. The atmosphere is shared by the marshes in Southern England to which, before the Continental shift, it was joined. The town and its environs have been too-much-fought-over not to be vaguely haunted.

Emma no longer went out; she had long periods of drunken torpor and if Horatia is to be believed, only once left her bed. It was Horatia who must go to the pawnshop, to shop in the cheapest market, and as the eventual bill proved, bring in wines and spirits, obtained on credit. They had no visitor but the priest.

The tourists had all gone home, but a few English remained, some in Emma's own predicament, some with duties to do, some for unspecified reasons. At the time a Mrs Hunter was living in Calais, and long after, but with interest in Lord Nelson and Lady Hamilton still lively, she told yet another biographer a very dramatic and self-glorifying tale, all about how she nursed Lady Hamilton, and provided food for her. It was myth. Other statements made by Mrs Hunter were easily disproved and Horatia said the whole story was false, and although Emma sometimes accused Horatia of telling lies, all her statements held together and had the ring of truth. 'The time I spent in Calais is too indelibly stamped on my memory ever to forget', she said. And since almost everything she said about Emma was tinged with compassion – not affection but pity and toleration, one feels that had Mrs Hunter been even half the angel of mercy she described herself to be, Horatia would have remembered her with gratitude.

Sometimes Emma was conscious and Horatia begged her to tell her who her mother was. By that time the well-kept secret was no longer a secret, but Horatia obviously longed for Emma to say something which would deny what the letters revealed. 'But she would not, influenced then I think by the fear that I might leave her.' Under questions, Emma turned irritable. 'For some time before her death she was not kind to me, but she had much to try her alas to spite her . . .'

Alone in one squalid room together; the woman, not yet fifty, the girl not yet fourteen, despite all the pretence. If Emma left her bed only once after the move into Calais, one can imagine what the girl's duties included, things made only tolerable to server and served by love, in this case lacking. Dogged conscientiousness, pity, tolerance, compassion, but no love.

Emma died on the 15th of January 1815. She had suffered physical ills, but her finally lethal complaint was a broken spirit. She had lost the will to live.

Mrs Hunter said that she made, out of a black silk petticoat, a shroud to cover the plain deal coffin; and that she ran around Calais trying to find an English clergyman and finally discovered an Irish officer on half-pay but for whose good offices Lady Hamilton would have been buried without any religious ceremony at all.

This sensational story was contradicted, not only by Horatia but by the accounts of the British Consul at the time, Mr Cadogan. Whether Horatia went to him on her own initiative, or whether Emma, in a lucid moment remembered how useful ambassadors and consuls could be to expatriots had directed her, we cannot know. Mr Cadogan and his wife took charge of everything. Emma was buried in an oak coffin, and the whole funeral, payment of priests and burial ground men, and candles, cost almost £29. Her last wish – that she should be buried in England, had to be disregarded because of the expense. The funeral was conducted according to the rites of the Roman Catholic Church and that would have been her wish; toward the end of her days in England she had been faintly drawn to Catholicism, and since coming to France had openly professed it.

Mr Cadogan paid what she owed for wines and spirits, £77: and he redeemed the poor articles which Horatia had pawned. It is pleasant to think that he was repaid in full.

Pleasant, too, to know that Horatia did at last go to Ashfold. Mr Matcham met her at Dover and took her home to be one of his family; she married happily and lived to be eighty. Another story . . .

There was one thing about the funeral which would have pleased Emma. She had been famous and sought after for her beauty; she had become notorious for the scandals attached to her name. She had been the intimate of one Queen, consistently snubbed by another. She had spent money lavishly, and given it away with a like openhandedness; she died in poverty, her very shawl in pawn. She had loved and served England, but she died in a foreign land. She might have had a pitiable funeral. But the master and captain of every English ship in the harbour of Calais that day put on his best clothes, came ashore and followed her to the grave. Stern, hard-bitten, sentimental men, not much concerned with gossip. Nelson was their hero, and she had been – would always be – his beloved Emma.

Illustration Acknowledgments

Figures in **bold** type, indicate pages opposite or between
which colour plates are to be found.

The following abbreviations are
used:

BL: British Library Board.
BM: Courtesy of the Trustees
of the British Museum.
DW: Derrick Witty.
GLC: Greater London Council,
Iveagh Bequest, Kenwood.
Mansell: Mansell Collection.
MEPL: Mary Evans Picture
Library.
MH: Michael Holford.
NMM: National Maritime
Museum, London.
NPG: National Portrait Gallery,
London.
NT: National Trust.
RTHPL: Radio Times Hulton
Picture Library.
RNM: Courtesy of the Royal
Naval Museum, Portsmouth.
TG: Tate Gallery, London.
V&A: Victoria and Albert
Museum, London.
WC: Courtesy of the Trustees,
The Wallace Collection,
London.

Frontispiece RNM
page 8–9 Mansell
11 RTHPL
12 NMM
13 RNM. Photo: DW
15 MEPL
16 GLC
17 Uppark/NT. Photo: John
Bethell
18 Mrs R. J. Meade-
Featherstonhaugh, Uppark.
Photo: Angelo Hornak
19 Uppark/NT
20 V&A. Photo: DW
20 *(inset)* From the collection at
Parham Park, Sussex

22–5 RTHPL
27 *(left)* GLC
27 *(right)* NPG
28 NMM
29 Mansell
32 BM. Photo: DW
32 NPG
33 (above) BL
33 (below) BM. Photo: MH
35–7 NMM
39 RTHPL
42 V&A. Photo: DW
44–5 MEPL
47 RNM. Photo: DW
48–9 Palazzo Reale, Caserta
50 RTHPL
53 NPG
55 RTHPL
57 BM. Photo: DW
60–4 NMM
68 *(left and right)* NMM
70 RTHPL
70–1 Mansell
72 Mr and Mrs Jack G. Taylor
of Austin, Texas
72–3 Anglesey Abbey/NT.
Photo: John Bethell
73 Museo di Capodimonte,
Naples. Photo: Scala
74 Mansell
77 RTHPL
79 *(left)* Mansell
79 *(right)* RTHPL
80–1 NMM
82 BM. Photo: John Freeman
84–5 RTHPL
88–9 Collection of Mrs C. A.
Robinson Jr., Rhode Island
91 RNM. Photo: DW
92–3 NMM
94 The Museum of London
95 MEPL
96 RTHPL
96–7 Mansell
99 NMM

100 BM. Photo: DW
104–7 NMM
109 RNM. Photo: DW
110–11 NMM. Photos: DW
112 *(above)* RTHPL
112–15 NMM
116 RTHPL
118 NMM. Photo: DW
120–1 WC
124–5 NMM. Photos: DW
127 *(top)* MEPL
127 *(bottom)* NMM. Photos: DW
129 NPG
132–5 NMM. Photos: DW
137 *(above)* NMM
137 *(right)* RNM. Photo: DW
138 NPG
140 NMM
142 BL
143 NMM
144 Mansell
145 NMM
146–7 RTHPL
149 NMM
150 Mansell
152–3 NMM. Photo: MH
152 & 153 NMM. Photos: DW
154 Mrs R. J. Meade-
Featherstonhaugh, Uppark.
Photo: DW
155 *(inset)* NPG
155 Richard Green Galleries
157 NMM
159 Mansell
165–7 RTHPL
172 *(left)* NMM
172 *(right)* RNM, McCarthy
Collection. Photos: DW
173 NMM
174 NPG
176–7 Mansell
180 The Museum of London
182 Private collection in USA.
Photo: Leger Galleries Ltd
183 V&A. Photo: DW

Index

Figures in **bold** type indicate pages opposite or between which colour plates are to be found; figures in *italics* indicate pages on which black-and-white illustrations appear.

B
Hamilton
Lofts
Emma Hamilton